A Learning Community Built on Strengths

A LEARNING COMMUNITY BUILT ON STRENGTHS:

Inspiring Educators to Positively Impact Student Lives

BY KATIE ALANIZ

ROWMAN & LITTLEFIELD
Lanham • Boulder • New York • London

Published by Rowman & Littlefield
An imprint of The Rowman & Littlefield Publishing Group, Inc.
4501 Forbes Boulevard, Suite 200, Lanham, Maryland 20706
www.rowman.com

86-90 Paul Street, London EC2A 4NE

British Library Cataloguing in Publication Information Available

Library of Congress Cataloging-in-Publication Data
Names: Alaniz, Katie, author.
Title: A learning community built on strengths: inspiring educators to positively impact student lives / by Katie Alaniz.
Description: Lanham, Maryland: Rowman & Littlefield, [2024] | Includes bibliographical references. | Summary: "This book is designed to equip and inspire current educators and those considering the profession of teaching as they seek to positively impact student lives for years to come"—Provided by publisher.
Identifiers: LCCN 2023047299 (print) | LCCN 2023047300 (ebook) | ISBN 9781475871685 (cloth: acid-free paper) | ISBN 9781475871692 (paperback: acid-free paper) | ISBN 9781475871708 (ebook)
Subjects: LCSH: Learning, Psychology of. | Teaching. | Instructional Systems—Design. | Teachers—In-service training—United States. | Teachers—Training of—United States.
Classification: LCC LB1775.A397 2024 (print) | LCC LB1775 (ebook) | DDC 370.15/23—dc23/eng/20231201
LC record available at https://lccn.loc.gov/2023047299
LC ebook record available at https://lccn.loc.gov/2023047300

♾™ The paper used in this publication meets the minimum requirements of American National Standard for Information Sciences—Permanence of Paper for Printed Library Materials, ANSI/NISO Z39.48-1992.

Contents

PREFACE

The inspiration for authoring this guidebook resulted from a number of memorable shared experiences. Through my years spent investing in students' lives, I realized a mutual calling to support learners from all walks of life in achieving success. I believe that every student holds the potential to excel in their pursuit of new learning endeavors, and I also believe that educators wield tremendous influence in shaping the trajectory of their students' lives.

I have witnessed increased engagement, heightened intrinsic motivation, and greater joy in learning when students benefit from a strengths-based approach to education. As teachers and educational leaders cultivate a culture of appreciating the strengths every student brings to new learning experiences, they sky is the limit. Learners delve more confidently and thoughtfully into each new opportunity for growth as they realize they hold the potential to bring unique gifts to their classroom learning community. I believe that as educators, we collectively owe it to our students to capitalize on strengths rather than focusing upon weaknesses. In doing so, strengths lead to new strengths, and weaknesses become powerful opportunities for growth.

The following guidebook signifies a culmination of tried-and-true frameworks for meaningful learning, incorporating key insights from previous guidebooks that address the relentless pursuit of purposeful academic endeavors for the benefit of students, both now and in the future (Wilson, Alaniz, & Sikora,

2016; Alaniz, 2021; Alaniz & Hao, 2022; Alaniz & Cerling, 2023).

As a lifelong learner who has consistently benefitted from the lasting impacts of strengths-focused teachers and mentors, as a passionate educator who has taught within diverse contexts covering first grade through doctoral programs, and as an individual who wholeheartedly believes that every student deserves to identify and capitalize on their giftings, I hold great confidence in the promises inherent within a strengths-based approach to teaching and learning.

Learning endeavors should be purposeful, exciting, and filled with joy—for both educators and their students. Strength-based approaches to education play a key role in meaningful and joyful teaching and learning. I hope and pray that this will be true for all who read this book and incorporate the principles within it.

In the words of renowned author C. S. Lewis, "There are far, far better things ahead than anything we leave behind." As we cultivate a life of focusing upon strengths, we naturally discover that the best is yet to be. There is always something greater ahead, and each day of learning entails new adventures in uncovering the best in our students, as well as the best in ourselves.

REFERENCES

Alaniz, K. (2021). *Collegial coaching: Mentoring for knowledge and skills that transfer to real-world applications.* Lanham, MD: Rowman & Littlefield Education.

Alaniz, K., & Cerling, K. (2023). *Authentic assessment in action: An everyday guide for bringing learning to life through meaningful assessment.* Lanham, MD: Rowman & Littlefield Education.

Alaniz, K., & Hao, D. (2022). *The maximizer mindset: Work less, achieve more, spread joy.* Lanham, MD: Rowman & Littlefield Education.

Wilson, D., Alaniz, K., & Sikora, J. (2016). *Digital media in today's classrooms: The potential for meaningful teaching, learning, and assessment.* Lanham, MD: Rowman & Littlefield Education.

Acknowledgments

This book is devoted to the glory of God and is dedicated to my incredible father, Robert ("Bob") Irvin Ellis, III (1952–2023). Dad's life provided a consistent reflection of the power of celebrating the best in others. He possessed an uncanny ability to focus on other's strengths and to intuitively inspire those within his life to reach their fullest potential. My heart is filled with gratitude for the priceless treasure of witnessing the profound impacts of this gift lived out in my father's life.

I would like to convey my heartfelt appreciation for my amazing husband Steven (a true hero and my number one cheerleader) and to my incredible family and friends for consistently providing tremendous encouragement and joining me in countless prayers through each new adventure.

I also want to express my sincere gratitude for educators throughout my life who inspired a love for lifelong learning within my heart through their willingness to recognize potential within me, even before I could see it myself. These include Dr. Dawn K. Wilson (my professor, dear friend, and mentor) and my very first teachers, my amazing dad and mom, Bob and Belinda Ellis. Their examples continue to inspire me in life and learning, every single day.

Introduction

In today's academic settings, educators face student issues that arise beyond the walls of the classroom while striving to reach learners who experience the world through varied lenses. They must be ready to support students with a myriad of unique learning differences as they engage with various content areas. This requires that teachers think beyond themselves, adjusting learning experiences to meet unpredictable needs of students with each new day.

What sets those teachers, who remain and thrive, apart from those who simply survive until another professional pursuit comes along? Are some individuals simply "born to teach" and others destined to eventually move on? Or could it be that those educators with remarkable staying power have learned the secret to sustained success over time?

A Learning Community Built on Strengths: Inspiring Educators to Positively Impact Student Lives is designed to equip and inspire current teachers and those considering the profession of teaching as they seek to positively impact student lives for years to come. In an age in which fewer and fewer educators view teaching as a lifelong profession, this book provides practical strategies for not only surviving but, even more so, for thriving as a teacher. The forthcoming chapters outline a transformative framework that empowers educators to foster a learning community built upon strengths.

When students receive feedback that addresses only gaps in their learning, they often intuitively begin performing in accordance with the low benchmarks set for them. This phenomenon embodies a self-fulfilling prophecy, in which the expectation for the behavior of a student brings the prophesied (expected) behavior to fruition. In today's world, there seems to be a pervasiveness of deficit-driven education. Many students eventually begin to believe that being smart equates to simply avoiding mistakes, and many educators measure and define success in narrow academic terms that often label incredibly bright and talented students as lacking intelligence.

Countless students are so zoned in on attempts to mitigate weakness that their strengths ultimately become neglected. This places them in a completely fixed mindset and sucks the love out of learning and of school. A strengths-based approach to teaching and learning is founded on what learners are able to achieve rather than areas of weakness. Chapter 1, "Addressing the State of Education Today: The Dangers of Deficit-Driven Teaching and Learning," sets the stage for the coming chapters through an overview of the "why" behind a strengths-based approach to education, offering an alternative to the more dangerous status quo of deficit-focused methods.

Chapter 2, "Focusing on the Best: The Relentless Pursuit of Strengths," examines why strengths-based teaching matters from the perspective of today's learners. The world within and beyond educational settings is portrayed through the eyes of Gen Z students, a group of learners with a practical eye toward the future. As they prepare for the extraordinary responsibility of inheriting our planet, they also long for meaningful, rewarding educational endeavors that will ready them for their future pursuits.

Today's students look forward to a professional landscape that values creativity, collaboration, critical thinking, global and digital citizenship, communication, and genuine character. Through embarking on a reflective journey in the shoes of today's students, this chapter sets the stage for understanding learners' diverse needs and interests to spark their motivation, engagement, and progress.

Focusing on students' strengths unlocks creativity! Focusing on deficits drives insecurity and discourages any type of risk-taking. Intentionally pinpointing and building upon strengths empowers them to accomplish more in less time versus expending a great deal of effort with minimal outcome, ultimately fighting an uphill battle. Like trying to be proficient in writing with a nondominant hand, much time and effort can be wasted. Focusing and capitalizing on strengths encourages teachers and learners to tap into and discover passions and purposes, whereas a deficient mindset inhibits this from happening.

In today's world, accessibility in educational settings is more important than ever as students with learning differences become less and less the outliers. Educators have a moral obligation to effectively address the needs of all students, and a strengths-based approach to teaching can profoundly support paradigm shifts toward accessibility for all learners.

Unless the unique potential of each student is brought to light in meaningful ways within classroom settings, opportunities for flourishing may be squandered. Chapter 3, "Celebrating Our Differences: Divergent Thinking as an Asset," overviews and expounds upon the power of neurodiversity in educational settings, explores a number of conditions considered neurodiverse, and offers practical applications for supporting neurodiverse students with skills needed for future success in life.

King Solomon of Israel, the beneficiary of unparalleled wisdom, famously remarked, "Two are better than one, because they have a good return for their labor: if either of them falls down, one can help the other up. But pity anyone who falls and has no one to help them up" (*New International Version*, 2011, Ecclesiastes 4:9–10). This wise principle applies to countless aspects of life, including educational settings.

In a world in which individualism is prized and teachers often work in silos, far too many educators overlook the power of connectivity. Chapter 4, "Capitalizing on Collaboration: Teamwork Makes the Dream Work," presents practical steps for discovering, developing, and capitalizing upon "perfect pairings" to cultivate student success, including partnerships with fellow colleagues. This chapter provides practical tools for building educators' capacity to collaborate with a community of learners who will make a strengths-based teaching paradigm happen. Strengths-based teaching and learning allow teachers and students to collaborate and add value to the learning experience for all. Once individuals within an organization learn to capitalize on strengths together, the magic of transformed educational experiences truly happens.

Students arrive to school with a variety of experiences and competencies. Thus, simultaneously teaching twenty to thirty students (or more) with maximum effectiveness can present quite the challenge. Chapter 5, "Tackling Technological Change: The Potential of Today's Innovative Educational Opportunities," focuses on how digital tools and resources in classroom environments can allow for differentiated as well as reciprocal learning, as students learn alongside and from one another.

Teachers must make a wide range of decisions when considering student-centered technology integration. Today's digital tools and resources can ultimately provide greater accessibility for all learners, regardless of unique learning styles and differences. Chapter 5 presents practical strategies for supporting learners in developing knowledge and skills for the digital age through purposeful technology integration.

As teachers face increasing demands for accountability and progressively limited time to spare, professional development may naturally be viewed as another box to check off on an extensive to-do list. Yet when educators facilitate reflective communities of practice that focus on strengths-based teaching and learning, they often find that their implementation of such approaches becomes more natural and purposeful, producing powerful results.

Chapter 6, "Embracing Lifelong Learning: The Power of Purposeful Professional Development," provides feasible strategies for cultivating strengths-based communities of practice in which such strategies can be explored, discussed, and built upon, ultimately impacting student lives for the better.

Although the United States is known for individuality, US school systems are surprisingly cookie-cutter in many ways. Education for the masses has created derivative approaches that may stifle students' creativity and progress in learning, placing students in categories with narrowly tailored metrics of intelligence that label and stigmatize them.

Considering how many schools operate, it would seem that the definitions of "intelligence" and "success" equate to making the fewest mistakes on often subjective and narrow measures. Chapter 7, "Reflecting on the Road Less Traveled: The Joy-filled Journey Ahead," offers practical steps for employing an individualized, strengths-based approach to education that provides avenues for student creativity to flourish and for students (and their teachers) to ultimately and joyfully reach their fullest potential.

REFERENCE

New International Version. (2011). BibleGateway.com. http://www.biblegateway .com/versions/New-International-Version-NIV-Bible/#booklist.

Addressing the State of Education Today

The Dangers of Deficit-Driven Teaching and Learning

Whether you think you can or you think you can't, you're right.
—HENRY FORD

TEACHING IS BOTH AN ART AND A SCIENCE. EDUCATORS DISPLAY artistry in connecting with learners and inspiring them to engage in classroom experiences. Simultaneously, they rely upon research-based instructional practices to support students in developing new knowledge and skills. Many believe that teaching is among the most rewarding professions while recognizing that it can also be among the most challenging.

Teachers may experience days, weeks, and even years when it seems as though setbacks press in from all sides, even despite the immeasurable time, thought, and effort they devote to their profession. They may face administrators who question why their entire class is not scoring in the desired percentile on exams, teammates who offer a "better way" of keeping the students in line, and parents who seem to believe that their child is the consistent exception to the rule.

Faced with pressing demands for accountability and relentless requests from stakeholders on all sides—not to mention the task of managing the academic, social-emotional, and physical well-being of potentially tens or hundreds of students each year—the increasing shortage of teachers seems more comprehensible.

Even still, those drawn to the profession of teaching persist in showing up day after day, motivated by the desire to impact students' lives for the better. They serve learners sometimes facing vastly different challenges than those of the past. In increasing numbers, today's students struggle to learn while dealing with such issues as poverty, abuse and neglect, homelessness, bullying (including cyberbullying), eating disorders, violence, pregnancy, drugs, suicide, and dropping out of school.

Educators face student issues that arise beyond the walls of the classroom while striving to reach learners who experience the world through a wide range of diverse viewpoints. They must be ready to support students with a myriad of unique learning differences as they engage with various content areas. This requires that teachers think beyond themselves, adjusting learning experiences to meet unpredictable needs of students with each new class.

What sets those teachers who remain and thrive apart from those who simply survive until another professional pursuit comes along? Are some individuals simply "born to teach" and others destined to eventually move on? Or could it be that those educators with remarkable staying power have learned the secret to sustained success over time?

The forthcoming chapters of this book are designed to equip and inspire current educators and those considering the profession of teaching as they seek to positively impact student lives for years to come. In an age in which fewer and fewer educators view teaching as a lifelong profession, this book provides practical strategies for not only surviving but, even more so, for thriving as a teacher.

The following pages outline a transformative framework that empowers educators to foster a learning community built upon strengths—strengths of students, the students' parents, colleagues, community members, and ultimately, strengths of the teachers themselves.

THE POWER OF THE SELF-FULFILLING PROPHECY

In 1948, Robert K. Merton, an American sociologist who is widely considered among the founding fathers of modern sociology, coined the term "self-fulfilling prophecy." In his words, the term describes "a false definition of the situation evoking a behavior which makes the originally false conception come true" (Merton, 1968, p. 477). In simple terms, self-fulfilling prophecies find their basis in misrepresentations of the truth or guesses about reality that ultimately bring hypothetical situations to life. This may occur as the result of innate psychological reactions to predictions and worries regarding the future.

Through his research, Merton (1968) observed that certain beliefs may bring about real-life consequences that cause a person's situation to mirror their beliefs. Oftentimes, those impacted by the self-fulfilling prophecy neglect to associate their beliefs with the resulting consequences they predicted or fearfully anticipated. These self-fulfilling prophecies may entail intrapersonal processes (such as a person's beliefs that impact their own behavior) and/or interpersonal processes (such as a person's beliefs that impact another's behavior).

Research has demonstrated that an individual's expectations for themselves impact various outcomes in their lives. Additionally, their expectations of others impact their thoughts, feelings, and actions toward those around them. A timeless experiment conducted in the 1960s by Robert Rosenthal and Lenore Jacobsen offered evidence to support this principle. Research findings from this study (and subsequent studies) demonstrated that teachers' expectations of students affected students' academic performance more significantly than differences in intelligence or talent.

Rosenthal and Jacobsen (1968) conducted their research within a public elementary school setting, where they selected a random group of student participants. The researchers told the children's teachers that this particular group of learners had taken the Harvard Test of Inflected Acquisition and that the results of the test identified them as "growth-spurters." The researchers next explained that these students held vast potential and could be expected to demonstrate significant intellectual growth over the coming year.

The researchers subsequently collected performance data on every student within the school and evaluated the "ordinary" students' academic gains in comparison to the academic gains of those in the growth-spurter group. Not surprisingly, those children the teachers anticipated to achieve significant gains (the randomly selected growth-spurters) ultimately demonstrated more extensive academic growth in comparison to their peers. Because the students were not informed of their false Test of Inflected Acquisition results, the explanation for these outcomes lies in the power of the teachers' expectation to impact the performance of learners within their classes.

This study portrays the power of the Pygmalion effect, the term used for a self-fulfilling prophecy relating to interpersonal processes. According to Rosenthal and Babad (1985), in instances in which individuals anticipate certain behaviors from others, they are likely to act in ways that increase the likelihood of the anticipated behavior by those around them.

Self-fulfilling prophecies naturally lead to powerful cycles of thought and behavior, and these cycles may bring about either positive or negative impacts upon a person's life. As individuals hold firmly to certain beliefs about themselves, they become more likely to behave in ways that align with those beliefs, thereby reinforcing the beliefs and fostering the same actions again and again.

This closely aligns with the potential impacts a person's beliefs about others may cause. When someone harbors strong beliefs about another person, they may behave in ways that encourage the other person to confirm those beliefs, thereby reinforcing the beliefs over time. As negative outcomes occur because of such cycles of beliefs and behaviors, the cycles may be referred to as "vicious cycles."

When individuals hold tightly to certain beliefs about themselves or others, those beliefs often impact their actions toward others. Such beliefs, whether true or untrue, may cause others to behave in ways that coincide with beliefs directed toward them, reinforcing the initial beliefs. Although vicious cycles such as this may appear in any number of contexts, they commonly exist within educational settings, holding the power to impact students' lives for years and years to come.

According to Rosenthal's classic studies of the Pygmalion effect, teachers may innately hold to preconceived beliefs about certain students without even realizing the presence of these beliefs. For example, they may assume that some learners are naturally intellectually gifted, associating them with a promising academic future. Within the same classroom, they may view others as inferior from an intellectual perspective or as students posing behavioral challenges.

In such cases, teachers may unintentionally treat students viewed as promising according to their beliefs, providing them with extra support and encouragement. On the other hand, they may treat students assumed to be challenging in ways that reflect these negative beliefs, instinctively determining that an investment of extra time and effort might be wasted, allowing them to slip by with subpar work.

Oftentimes, students' views of themselves begin to mirror their teachers' views of them. Learners viewed as full of potential begin to feel confident in their academic abilities and may become more highly motivated to succeed. Alternatively, students viewed as intellectually inferior or troublesome may begin to see little point in striving to excel academically or to exhibit commendable behavior in class.

Although the cycle of self-fulfilling prophecies may positively impact students viewed as promising, it can be highly detrimental for students viewed as academically unprepared or behaviorally challenged. When students receive feedback that addresses only gaps in their learning, they often intuitively begin performing in accordance with the low benchmarks set for them.

This phenomenon embodies a self-fulfilling prophecy within educational contexts in which the expectation for the behavior of a student brings the prophesied behavior to fruition. In today's world, there seems to be a pervasiveness of deficit-driven education. Many students eventually begin to believe that being smart equates to simply avoiding mistakes. Many educators measure and define success in narrow academic terms that often label incredibly bright and talented students as lacking intelligence.

THE VICIOUS CYCLE CONTINUES

Self-fulfilling prophecies are certainly not limited to educational contexts. Yet patterns of thought related to self-fulfilling prophecies that take root even at a very young age within school settings may easily impact the remainder of a person's life. Consider the hypothetical story of Truman and Sam, two students who began Mrs. Johnson's kindergarten class during the same academic year.

The summer before kindergarten was spent quite differently by each boy. Truman's parents invested hours in preparing him for the year to come, reading books with him throughout each evening after their workday ended, touring various museums with him over the weekends, and consistently reinforcing the notion that school would prove to be an exciting adventure through countless conversations with him. As a result, Truman eagerly awaited his first day of school, looking forward to borrowing new books from the school library and to learning more about

6

the massive dinosaur specimens he first encountered in the local museum of natural sciences.

Sam's summer before kindergarten shaped up to be completely different than Truman's. By no fault of their own, Sam's parents found themselves needing to work multiple jobs and long hours to make ends meet; as much as they longed to spend time preparing Sam for his first year in school, they found little time to do so. Their exhausting work schedules left very few opportunities for reading with Sam or discussing his upcoming start to kindergarten. Sam felt uncertain about what to expect from kindergarten and faced his start to school with a slight sense of trepidation.

On the first day of class, Truman walked confidently into Mrs. Johnson's class, eager for his kindergarten journey to officially commence. When Mrs. Johnson invited the class to select a book from the classroom library while waiting for the first lesson to begin, Truman excitedly selected a book he recognized from his home bookshelf—one he knew the words to by heart after reading it so many times before bed with his parents.

On that day, as Sam entered Mrs. Johnson's classroom, he experienced the sensation of butterflies in his stomach for the first time. He felt unsure of his ability to perform well in school and wondered if others in his class might know information he did not. When Mrs. Johnson asked him to select a book from the classroom library, he felt uncertain about the best book to choose. None of the books looked familiar, and he did not yet know how to read or even how to begin trying. He noticed that a boy the teacher referred to as "Truman" seemed to be happily and confidently reading a book from the library.

As Sam stood within the little classroom library, he wistfully gazed at Truman's seamless demonstration of advanced reading abilities, wondering how he might become like Truman. Sam's thoughts were interrupted by Mrs. Johnson's eager declaration: "I see that some of you have already selected a book! Truman, I am proud of you for reading so quietly!"

As Mrs. Johnson circulated throughout the room, she approached Sam in the classroom library. "Sam, I noticed that you haven't yet followed instructions. I asked you to select a book, and you're letting time pass you by as you're standing in the library."

Sam felt his cheeks grow warm as a sense of embarrassment flooded over him. "I don't know which book to pick. I don't know how to read."

"That's okay," Mrs. Johnson replied. "You can select any book you'd like. Most students don't come to kindergarten knowing how to read. You will learn."

Sam felt relief as Mrs. Johnson encouraged him. Yet he still found himself gazing back at Truman, steadfastly reading his chosen book with a pronounced sense of joy. Mrs. Johnson noticed Sam's gaze and quietly remarked, "Only very few of your classmates are already reading. Truman is a very advanced reader, but not everyone will read as easily as Truman does."

Mrs. Johnson intended to reassure Sam, but it was in that moment that he (and Mrs. Johnson) began to believe that Sam may not be one of the more promising students. And, although Mrs. Johnson had not intended for other students to overhear her conversation with Sam, Truman had picked up on Mrs. Johnson's compliment of his reading abilities. He felt assured (as did Mrs. Johnson) that he would naturally excel in school.

The first week of class, Mrs. Johnson divided the students into reading groups bearing the names of various animals. There were the bears, the dolphins, the penguins, the blue jays, and a random assortment of other animals. She intentionally did not name the groups by letter (A, B, C, D, etc.) in hopes of avoiding students' notice of her groupings by ability. Yet it was obvious to Sam (and to others) that the most advanced readers, such as Truman, were placed in the dolphin and blue jay groups; the struggling readers, including Sam, were placed in the bear and penguin groups.

Sam also noticed that Mrs. Johnson approached the groups a bit differently. When she worked with dolphins and blue jays, her cheery face and elevated pitch of voice typically expressed enthusiasm regarding their progress. When she approached the bears and penguins, her more serious face, while still kind, often conveyed slight concern. Her tone was not as upbeat, and she sometimes seemed a bit fatigued when offering extra support.

Although Sam worked diligently to improve his reading abilities, he could tell by Mrs. Johnson's nonverbal and verbal cues that he was lagging behind. By the conclusion of his kindergarten year, he could no longer fight the nagging thought that he might never achieve success in school. For him, school would be more about surviving than thriving.

He and Truman continued to move through the grades together, and they eventually became close friends. Sam admired Truman's seemingly natural ability to excel in school, and yet he struggled with the sense that this level of success was out of reach for him personally. Sam often dreaded school, fully expecting that each day would be filled with seemingly insurmountable challenges.

On the other hand, Truman enjoyed school, and he found that teachers seemed to appreciate having him in class. By and large, Truman viewed teachers as trusted sources of support, and he benefitted from encouraging and helpful interactions with them. However, he felt saddened (and a slight tinge of guilt) when he noticed that his friend Sam did not receive the same enthusiastic treatment from some teachers. The fact that a number of teachers noticeably drew different conclusions about Truman and Sam even before the first quiz or exam bothered both boys year after year.

Truman and Sam moved through middle school and high school together, determined to attend the same university upon graduation. Truman was poised to graduate as valedictorian, confident that he would be admitted to his top university choice, a select Ivy League school. Sam was a B and C student; although Truman consistently assured Sam that his extracurricular activities and excellence in sports would make up for his lack of As, Sam had his own doubts.

As the boys prepared their college applications and wrote the corresponding essays, Truman's heart soared with great expectations regarding his probable Ivy League future. Simultaneously, Sam felt overcome with doubts about the chances of him even being accepted to college, let alone the prestigious university Truman had in mind.

The boys submitted their applications on the same day. As Truman eagerly awaited his acceptance letter, Sam anxiously awaited his rejection letter. Low and behold, when the letters arrived in their mailboxes several months later, both Truman and Sam were proven correct. Truman and his family planned a massive celebration to mark the conclusion to a highly successful grade school career and the beginning of the rest of his life of academic and professional success.

Truman felt a familiar tinge of sadness and guilt as he handed Sam an invitation to the party. As he consistently had over the years, Sam expressed sincere admiration for Truman and planned to wholeheartedly celebrate Truman's most recent success. At the same time, Sam once again settled into the familiar feeling he had initially experienced on his first day of kindergarten. As he, Mrs. Johnson, and many of his teachers after her had accepted, he would never find success in school. He was grateful simply to have survived his grade school years.

Truman and Sam committed to staying in touch as Truman prepared to embark on his journey to the university of his dreams while Sam prepared to take an open position as a server at a popular local restaurant. As Truman's academic and professional aspirations were accomplished one by one, Sam felt content for the opportunity to work his way toward promotion from server to manager at the restaurant where he worked.

Truman and Sam often met for dinner when Truman returned to his hometown on weekends and during holiday seasons. During one return visit, as Sam was conversing with Truman about his favorite courses, Sam earnestly asked, "How does it feel to consistently succeed in school? I've always thought of you as unstoppable when it comes to academics."

Without hesitation, Truman replied, "I guess I felt set up for success from the very beginning. Remember Mrs. Johnson's class? It was like she just knew I was going to do well in school. . . . Almost as though there was no other option for me. It was a done deal." Truman paused for a moment to grab another french fry from his plate and nonchalantly continued, "You know you're just as smart as I am, right? Honestly, you're probably smarter. I've always admired how quickly you learned the plays Coach Kelly wanted us to memorize for football, or how you literally won every single chess game we ever played. That takes brains. It always made me sad that you just kind of assumed that school wasn't meant for you."

Sam listened intently to Truman's words, both encouraged by Truman's reassurance regarding Sam's intelligence, while equally discouraged that school never seemed to work out for him. As he had many times in the past, Sam silently pondered the "why" behind his struggles in school. It would not be until years later that he fully realized and ultimately accepted how profoundly various self-fulfilling prophesies, brought about by teachers and by himself, had impacted the entire trajectory of his life.

FROM SURVIVING TO THRIVING

Although the story of Truman and Sam is purely hypothetical, life experiences such as this happen far too often within today's educational settings. Teachers, administrators, and parents—even when thoroughly well-intentioned—are only human. By nature, human beings innately form beliefs that lead to self-fulfilling prophesies, every day, in countless contexts, including educational contexts. Even the most seemingly innocuous assumptions hold the power to ultimately alter the trajectory of a person's life. And this can happen at surprisingly young ages.

Most people can readily recall an instance in which the words spoken by a teacher—even the best teacher—impacted the way they approached school. Whether in kindergarten or senior year of high school, a teachers' words—as well as the looks given and the tone of voice used—carry tremendous weight with students. While an encouraging and appropriately challenging teacher may cause a student to adopt the mindset that success in school is attainable, even a single instance of discouragement or comparison to other students can significantly impact a student's belief in their ability to succeed.

How many students view their schooling journey as a test of survival rather than an opportunity to thrive as a learner? How many teachers view their teaching journey as a test of survival rather than an opportunity to thrive as an educator? In today's test-driven educational world, it can seem quite challenging to focus on possibilities beyond passing the next exam. When a great deal of time within educational settings is devoted to selecting the one right answer to each question asked, attention is naturally drawn to avoiding mistakes at all costs.

Modern educational systems in the United States easily divide learners into the "haves" and the "have nots." Students who enter school settings prepared for success are applauded for their ability to succeed and encouraged in this journey. Students who enter school settings without as much preparation for success may find that such great focus is placed on their learning deficits that it ultimately becomes hard to reverse this paradigm. Teachers between grade levels instinctively discuss the rising class of learners, and even before the first day of school, assumptions form that ultimately reinforce the growth, achievement, and success (or lack thereof) of certain students.

As a result, countless students are so zoned in on attempts to mitigate weakness, their strengths ultimately become neglected.

This places them in a completely fixed mindset and sucks the love out of learning and of school. Even prior to entering higher education settings, students must jump through so many hoops before they begin exploring and diving into their greatest interests. Education naturally becomes more about surviving than about thriving.

The great news is that there is an alternative. Any and every student holds the potential to excel in school. Yet the picture of what excelling looks like must be shifted. While deficit-focused educational methods concentrate on pinpointing weaknesses and eliminating them, strengths-based approaches emphasize the unique strengths each student brings to new learning experiences. A strengths-based approach to teaching and learning is founded in what learners can achieve rather than areas of weakness. This approach, which will be explored in depth in the coming chapters, offers an alternative to the more dangerous status quo of deficit-focused methods.

QUESTIONS FOR REFLECTION

Each day contains exactly 24 hours—that's 1,440 minutes. A relatively small investment of 15 to 30 minutes per day devoted to deeply, genuinely reflecting on the following questions will undoubtedly reap long-lasting dividends. Heartfelt reflection fuels the journey toward developing a learning community built on strengths, positively impacting the lives of countless students. The more honest each answer, the greater the potential impact. Now is the time to positively impact the state of education today, one learner at a time!

- In your academic, professional, and/or personal life, have you ever experienced the power of a self-fulfilling prophecy or a series of self-fulfilling prophecies? If so, how did this play out?

- As you reflect upon the hypothetical story of Truman and Sam, which of the characters in the story do you most identify with. Why?

- As you reflect upon Truman's and Sam's journeys, which of the students' journeys do you believe the learners under your influence most identify with. Why?

- Are you able to think of any students who seem so zoned in on attempts to mitigate weakness that their strengths ultimately become neglected? How does this mindset impact their opportunities for growth?

- What causes some students to be fearful of failure? Do you ever find yourself fearing failure? Why?

- As a student, did you typically experience a deficit-focused or strengths-based approach to education? How did this impact your view of school and your view of yourself as a learner? How does this impact your current approach to working with students?

ESSENTIAL IDEAS TO REMEMBER

Unfortunately, self-fulfilling prophecies run rampant within today's educational contexts. Far too often, expectations for students' behaviors bring the prophesied behaviors to fruition. Whether they originate with parents, teachers, the students themselves, or a combination of these factors, self-fulfilling prophesies and deficit-driven education are pervasive. Students may eventually latch onto the idea that intelligence equates to their ability to avoid mistakes. Educators may view success in limited academic terms that pigeonhole bright and talented students as unprepared or struggling.

Yet, there is a better path forward. The coming chapters explore strengths-based approaches to education through research, stories, and practical strategies. An exciting adventure awaits teachers and educational leaders seeking to cultivate a learning community built on strengths. The process of fostering such a community naturally inspires educators and their students, impacting lives for the better in countless ways. Let the adventure of strengths-based teaching and learning begin!

REFERENCES

Merton, R. K. (1948). The self-fulfilling prophecy. *The Antioch Review*, *8*(2), 193–210.

Rosenthal, R., and Babad, E. Y. (1985). Pygmalion in the gymnasium. *Educational Leadership*, *43*, 36–39.

Rosenthal, R., & Jacobson, L. (1968). Pygmalion in the classroom. *The Urban Review*, *3*, 16–20.

Focusing on the Best

The Relentless Pursuit of Strengths

*If I were to summarize in one sentence the single most import-
ant principle I have learned in the field of interpersonal
relations, it would be this:
Seek first to understand, then to be understood. This principle
is the key to effective interpersonal communication.*

—STEVEN COVEY

IN HIS TIMELESS, FREQUENTLY QUOTED BOOK *THE 7 HABITS OF
Highly Effective People: Restoring the Character Ethic*, Covey
(1989) outlines priceless life principles that apply to countless
personal and professional endeavors. Among these principles,
Habit 5 points to the value of seeking first to understand, which
forms a foundational and essential component of strengths-based
approaches to education. In fact, unless teachers and educational
leaders adopt this habit within their professional practices, a
strengths-based approach to education is simply unattainable.
The implementation of this habit represents a first and vital
step toward strengths-based teaching and learning.

In the book *Authentic Assessment in Action: An Everyday
Guide for Bringing Learning to Life through Meaningful Assessment,*

Alaniz and Cerling (2023) describe advantages and challenges of applying the habit of seeking first to understand to differences among generations:

> Whether yearning for departed days or longing for the passage of time, everyone shares something in common. . . . They were at one time a member of the newest generation—the generation being surveyed, studied, questioned, critiqued, and/or applauded. No matter the generation, individuals of each age group face certain generalizations, assumptions, and scrutiny. As members of older generations attempt to understand those in their younger years, the temptation to marvel and criticize sometimes weighs heavier than the desire to seek first to understand. This compulsion represents a natural part of life, as one generation views the world from a different lens than the next. Albert Einstein once remarked, "The trouble with the younger generation is that they don't stay young for very long." For far too many, the passage of time happens far too quickly. (pp. 1–2)

Within today's world, as digital innovations cause accelerated rates of change, the growing chasms between generations make a great deal of sense. As described by Alaniz and Cerling (2023),

> In considering life in the 1800s and earlier, for example, it becomes clear that developments in society progressed much more slowly in bygone years. Centuries ago, individuals from even two or three generations were more likely to maintain comparable lifestyles. In more recent years, social and technological innovations have caused the lifestyles of individuals from one generation to the next to vary more dramatically than in the past. As a result, a deficiency of intergenerational understanding has impacted today's educational institutions, corporations, non-profit organizations, government agencies, social settings, and nearly every other area of society, including varying cyberspheres. . . . In a digitally minded and globally interconnected world, these ramifications may easily span far

beyond an isolated disagreement between a Gen X parent and
Gen Z teenager. (p. 2)

Gen Z learners often have a practical eye toward the future. As
they prepare for the extraordinary responsibility of inheriting
our planet, they also long for meaningful, rewarding educational
endeavors that will ready them for their future pursuits. Yet, the
future they face will likely look very different than the future faced
by learners of the past. For example, as opposed to past expectations regarding the pursuit of one steady career, Gen Z students
will occupy approximately twenty jobs on average over the course
of their lifetimes. They often seek relevance and flexibility in academic and professional pursuits.

They foresee a professional landscape that embraces collaboration, communication, creativity, critical thinking, digital and
global citizenship, and sincere character. Many will ultimately
pursue career opportunities not yet invented. A study conducted
by Dell Technologies and the Institute for the Future (2018)
predicts that 85 percent of the jobs that will exist in 2030 were
not in existence in 2018. Through the collaboration of twenty
experts from across the globe, the study sought to determine how
emerging digital technologies (e.g., artificial intelligence and the
Internet of things) will ultimately shift humankind's modes of
working and living in 2030.

It may seem astonishing—if not impossible—to imagine that
85 percent of the job opportunities that will exist in 2030 had
not yet been conceived of in 2018. Yet considering the number of
professions today that did not yet exist fifteen to twenty years ago,
this prediction seems more feasible.

Viable career paths such as an app developer, social media
manager, cloud-computing specialist, and even influencer, now
allow individuals to earn significant sources of income, often
completely from the flexibility of their own homes. Even a couple
of decades ago, few could have imagined that this would someday

be the case. Although professional settings have experienced dramatic shifts over the last couple of decades, this pace of change has not been mirrored in school settings.

In fact, even when reflecting upon the last couple of centuries, this reality becomes especially apparent. With the turn of the twentieth century, public schools embraced widely popularized academic "innovations" corresponding with leading educational theories of the day. Educational researchers and leaders emphasized the value of efficiency, and broader goals focused on "mass-producing" students proficient in basic reading, computing, and writing. As described in the book *How People Learn*:

> In the early 1900s, the challenge of providing mass education was seen by many as analogous to mass production in factories. School administrators were eager to make use of the "scientific" organization of factories to structure efficient classrooms. Children were regarded as raw materials to be efficiently processed by technical workers (the teachers) to reach the end product (Bennett & LeCompte, 1990; Callahan, 1962; Kliebard, 1975). This approach attempted to sort the raw materials (the children) so that they could be treated somewhat as an assembly line. Teachers were viewed as workers whose job was to carry out directives from their superiors—the efficiency experts of schooling (administrators and researchers). (National Academies of Sciences, Engineering, and Medicine, 2000, p. 132)

Furthermore, these principles brought about deeply rooted influences upon assessment methods, moving the needle toward the dawn of standardized testing:

> The emulation of factory efficiency fostered the development of standardized tests for measurement of the "product," of clerical work by teachers to keep records of costs and progress (often at the expense of teaching), and of "management" of teaching by central district authorities who had little knowledge of

educational practice or philosophy (Callahan, 1962). In short, the factory model affected the design of curriculum, instruction, and assessment in schools. (National Academies of Sciences, Engineering, and Medicine, 2000, p. 132)

Unfortunately for today's students, many educational contexts have not kept pace with changes occurring in modern professional settings. In fact, educational institutions often lag far behind, with key decision makers continuing to cling to outdated ideals regarding "success" in learning. In the current digital age, the knowledge and skills necessary for success in groundbreaking professional contexts vastly differ from the knowledge and skills sought over the past centuries.

AS THE WHEEL OF TIME TURNS . . .

Now more than ever before, professional environments transform as technological innovations develop, necessitating a consistent reskilling of the workforce and an ever-changing job market. In a rapidly morphing professional landscape, educators within today's schools face the challenge of readying learners for forthcoming job opportunities not currently in existence.

While it is impossible to determine exactly the types of jobs students will someday pursue, teachers can empower leaners to embrace and acquire skills that will be valuable in any professional endeavor—even within those job opportunities not yet invented. Instead of focusing upon a mass production, standardized approach, future-focused learning experiences center on real-life applications.

Today's students crave experiences that are applicable to life beyond the walls of the classroom. They come alive when given the chance to build skills that will be useful as they pursue their future professional and personal aspirations. Such skills, which will ultimately be needed in countless professional contexts—even those not yet invented—include the "Six Cs" of learning in the digital age, originally described within a white paper written by Fullan and Scott (2014):

- Character: "Qualities of the individual essential for being personally effective in a complex world, including grit, tenacity, perseverance, resilience, reliability, and honesty."
- Citizenship: "Thinking like global citizens, considering global issues based on a deep understanding of diverse values with genuine interest in engaging with others to solve complex problems that impact human and environmental sustainability."
- Collaboration: "The capacity to work interdependently and synergistically in teams with strong interpersonal and team-related skills including effective management of team dynamics, making substantive decisions together, and learning from and contributing to the learning of others."
- Communication: "Mastery of three fluencies: digital, writing, and speaking tailored for a range of audiences."
- Creativity: "Having an 'entrepreneurial eye' for economic and social opportunities, asking the right questions to generate novel ideas, and demonstrating leadership to pursue those ideas into practice."
- Critical Thinking: "Critically evaluating information and arguments, seeing patterns and connections, construction meaningful knowledge and applying it in the real world" (pp. 6–7).

When learning opportunities focus on developing applicable skills rather than students' test-taking abilities, these experiences more naturally spark the motivation, engagement, and progress of all learners, instead of catering only to those who excel at test-taking strategies. Such educational endeavors allow learners' strengths to shine through while unlocking their creative abilities. Alternatively, focusing on deficits—particularly test-taking deficits—drives students' insecurity and discourages any type of risk-taking.

In the words of Alaniz and Cerling (2023),

> Considering today's ever-changing professional landscape, the process of developing basic numeracy, literacy, and content knowledge is not enough to prepare learners for the future they will face beyond their schooling years. Preparation for the future begins today. In order for students to be capable of navigating the complex world they will inherit, they must be able to create successfully, think critically, communicate effectively, collaborate skillfully, and consistently demonstrate citizenship and character. Rather than simply recalling what they have memorized for a quiz or test, they must be able to apply the knowledge and skills they have acquired to future academic, professional, and personal endeavors. (pp. 17–18)

STARTING WITH WHY AND BEGINNING WITH THE END IN MIND

In the inspiring book *Start with Why: How Great Leaders Inspire Everyone to Take Action*, Simon Sinek (2011) expounds on the truth that while most organizations can readily explain WHAT they do, and even though some can also articulate HOW they are better or unique, few can effectively describe WHY they do what they do.

In light of the practical nature of Gen Z students, they typically develop and maintain greater motivation when embarking on pursuits with a clear WHY in mind. Whether through educational, professional, or personal endeavors, meaningful experiences tied to real-world applications spark persistence and growth from today's students, not to mention increased buy-in. Educators who start with WHY support students in explicitly identifying the practical reasons for engaging in new learning experiences, even before the journey has begun.

The principle of "start with WHY" is also closely aligned with Covey's (1989) Habit 2 in *The 7 Habits of Highly Effective People: Restoring the Character Ethic*: "Begin with the end in mind." Insightful and innovative individuals prepare for new adventures in life by first reflecting upon the ultimate destination. It would not be wise to start packing for a trip without considering what the destination will be like. Similarly, today's pragmatic students desire to begin new learning endeavors with an end goal or goals in mind.

Sinek (2011) explains,

> Knowing your WHY is not the only way to be successful, but it is the only way to maintain a lasting success and have a greater blend of innovation and flexibility. When a WHY goes fuzzy, it becomes much more difficult to maintain the growth, loyalty and inspiration that helped drive the original success. By difficult, I mean that manipulation rather than inspiration fast becomes the strategy of choice to motivate behavior. This is effective in the short term but comes at a high cost in the long term. (p. 50)

Educators effectively inspire long-term persistence and achievement among learners, as well as intrinsic motivation, when they allow the WHY to be the focus of educational endeavors, beginning each new learning journey with the end in mind. The most effective teachers not only exhibit mindfulness regarding the WHY for new learning experiences, they also consistently discuss this WHY with their students. Even more significantly, they encourage and support students in developing and articulating WHYs of their own.

In doing so, they cultivate a learning environment in which lasting buy-in and growth from students—even once reluctant or apparently unmotivated learners—appear more intuitively and more frequently. When students find personal meaning and applications in their learning, they will more readily engage with their teacher, their classmates, and the various tools and resources available for learning.

Stellar educators support students in clearly pinpointing and articulating the chosen destination prior to starting any new learning journey. Such teachers design and introduce every unit and lesson by beginning with the end in mind and maintaining an awareness and emphasis upon the WHY. In doing so, they more successfully encourage authentic engagement from learners, as well as truly meaningful, applicable learning experiences.

QUESTIONS FOR REFLECTION

Each day contains exactly 24 hours—that's 1,440 minutes. A relatively small investment of 15 to 30 minutes per day devoted to deeply, genuinely reflecting on the following questions will undoubtedly reap long-lasting dividends. Heartfelt reflection fuels the journey toward developing a learning community built on strengths, positively impacting the lives of countless students. The more honest each answer, the greater the potential impact. Now is the time to focus on the best!

- Can you recall a time when you were a student and a teacher from a previous generation sought to appreciate your unique characteristics? If so, how did this impact you at that time?
- How do today's students respond to learning experiences that empower them to develop Fullan and Scott's (2014) "Six Cs" (listed below)? Why do you believe this to be the case?
  - Character
  - Citizenship
  - Collaboration
  - Communication

- Creativity
- Critical Thinking

- In your own words, why is it important that teachers start with WHY when introducing new concepts to students? How does this impact their learning?
- As you focus on the WHY when interacting with students, how does this impact your feelings about your work as an educator?

ESSENTIAL IDEAS TO REMEMBER

Focusing upon and capitalizing on strengths encourages teachers and students to tap into and discover passions and purposes, whereas a deficient mindset inhibits this from happening. Through embracing a reflective journey and placing themselves in the shoes of today's learners, educators more naturally gain students' attention and willingness to learn. Those teachers who remain mindful of students' interests and needs position themselves to encourage increased engagement and intrinsic motivation from their learners.

As educators start with WHY, learning becomes more focused on real-world applicability. As the WHY drives instructional endeavors, learning takes on new meaning for students. By beginning with the end in mind, contemplating the destination of each learning endeavor, and encouraging students to follow suit, teachers prime their students to find greater purpose and benefits in learning. Rather than students feeling that they are merely tagging along through each unit and lesson introduced, they begin to feel empowered to grasp and articulate the WHY behind their learning. In doing so, students transition from passive consumers of new information to active participants in an exciting learning journey—a journey they will not soon forget.

References

Alaniz, K. (2021). *Collegial coaching: Mentoring for knowledge and skills that transfer to real-world applications*. Lanham, MD: Rowman & Littlefield Education.

Alaniz, K., & Cerling, K. (2023). *Authentic assessment in action: An everyday guide for bringing learning to life through meaningful assessment*. Lanham, MD: Rowman & Littlefield Education.

Bennett, K. P., & LeCompte, M. D. (1990). *The way schools work: A sociological analysis of education*. New York: Longman.

Callahan, R. E. (1962). *Education and the cult of efficiency*. Chicago: University of Chicago Press.

Covey, S. R. (1989). *The 7 habits of highly effective people: Restoring the character ethic*. New York: Free Press.

Dell Technologies. (2018). "Realizing 2030: A divided vision of the future." https://bit.ly/2FvF1yi.

Fullan, M., & Scott, G. (2014). *New pedagogies for deep learning whitepaper: Education PLUS. Seattle, WA: Collaborative Impact SPC*.

Kliebard, H. M. (1975). Metaphorical roots of curriculum design. In *Curriculum Theorizing: The Reconceptualists*, W. Pinar, ed. Berkeley, CA: McCutchan.

National Academies of Sciences, Engineering, and Medicine. (2000). *How people learn: Brain, mind, experience, and school: expanded edition*. Washington, DC: The National Academies Press. https://doi.org/10.17226/9853.

Sinek, S. (2011). *Start with why*. Harlow, England: Penguin Books.

CHAPTER 3

Celebrating Our Differences

Divergent Thinking as an Asset

If everyone is thinking alike, then somebody isn't thinking.
—GEORGE S. PATTON

IN TODAY'S WORLD, ACCESSIBILITY IN EDUCATIONAL SETTINGS IS more important than ever before, as students with learning differences become less and less the outliers. Educators have a moral obligation to effectively address the needs of every student, and a strengths-based approach to teaching can profoundly support paradigm shifts toward accessibility for all learners. Unless the unique potential of each student is brought to light in meaningful ways within classroom settings, opportunities for flourishing may be squandered. This chapter overviews and expounds on the power of neurodiversity in educational contexts.

Prior to grasping the power of neurodiversity, it is essential to develop a common definition of this key term. A variety of viewpoints regarding neurodiversity exist today. Initially, Singer (1999) used the term "neurodiversity" as a means of revising the label "autistic spectrum disorder." Fellow scholars subsequently utilized "neurodiverse" to describe individuals with specific learning difficulties (Baker, 2011). Yet according to Lewis and Norwich (2004), a neurodiversity approach entails an understanding that "special needs" categories contain significant variations.

Seldom do these categories exist in isolation; instead, they often occur in combination with additional learning differences, sometimes referred to as "comorbidity" (Gilger & Kaplan, 2001) or "co-occurrence" (Jones & Kindersley, 2013). A neurodiversity approach finds its basis in the basic notion that everyone is neurodiverse, that normal human variations include learning differences, and that these variations represent vital components of a human ecosystem (Griffiths, 2020).

In his book *The Power of Neurodiversity: Unleashing the Advantages of Your Differently Wired Brain*, Dr. Thomas Armstrong (2011), executive director of the American Institute for Learning and Human Development, criticizes what he views as an expanding "culture of disabilities." The book effectively debunks the perspective that individuals with autism, attention deficit disorder, and dyslexia are somehow "defective." According to Armstrong, far too many within society have become single-minded in a "disease-based orientation" when considering brain-based differences, and there is a pressing need to uncover positive viewpoints to rectify this imbalanced approach.

Rather than being viewed as exhibiting problematic tendencies, Armstrong contends that people with "differently wired" brains should be seen as "neurodiverse." Such individuals should be recognized for how neurodiversity empowers them to excel in ways that might not otherwise be possible. Armstrong anticipates, in fact, that "normal" will ultimately become an antiquated concept as greater understandings develop regarding the uniqueness of each human being's brain. Considering his perspective that neurodiversity should be viewed as an asset instead of a deficit, Armstrong outlines eight key principles of neurodiversity throughout *The Power of Neurodiversity*.

Armstrong (n.d.) summarized these principles as follows for the American Institute for Learning and Human Development:

1. **The Human Brain Works More Like an Ecosystem than a Machine**. Up until now, the most often used metaphor to refer to the brain has been a computer (or some other type of machine). However, the human brain isn't hardware or software, it's wetware. The characterization of the brain as an unbelievably intricate network of ecosystems is much closer to the truth than that of a complex machine. We should devise a discourse that better reflects this new conception of the brain.

2. **Human Brains Exist Along Continuums of Competence**. Rather than regarding disability categories as discrete entities, it's more appropriate to speak of spectrums or continuums of competence. Recent research, for example, indicates that dyslexia is part of a spectrum that includes normal reading ability. Similarly, we use terms such as autistic spectrum disorders to suggest that there are different gradations of social ability that merge ultimately with normal behavior. This suggests that we are all somewhere along continuums related to literacy, sociability, attention, learning, and other cognitive abilities, and thus all of us are connected to each other rather than being separated into "normal" and "those having disabilities."

3. **Human Competence is Defined by the Values of the Culture to Which You Belong**. Categories of disability often deeply reflect the values of a culture. Dyslexia, for example, is based upon the social value that everyone be able to read. One hundred and fifty years ago, this wasn't the case, and dyslexia was unknown. Similarly, autism may reflect the cultural value that suggests that it's better to be in a relationship than to be alone. We should recognize that diagnostic categories are not purely scientifically based but reflect these deeper social biases.

4. **WhetherYou are Regarded as Disabled or Gifted Depends Largely on When and Where You Were Born**. In other times and other places, there have been different disability/ability diagnoses depending upon cultural values. In pre-Civil War America, for example, there was a disorder called "drapetomania" said to afflict blacks. Its meaning was "an obsession with the urge to flee one's slave masters" and reflected its racist roots. In India, today, there are people who would be labeled in the West as schizophrenic, but who are regarded as holy beings by the local population. We should not regard diagnostic labels as absolute and set in stone, but think, instead, of their existence relative to a particular social setting.

5. **Success in Life is Based on Adapting One's Brain to the Needs of the Surrounding Environment**. Despite Principles 3 and 4, however, it's true that we don't live in other places or times, consequently the immediate need is to adapt to our current contemporary culture. This means that a dyslexic person needs to learn how to read, an autistic individual needs to learn how to relate to others socially, a schizophrenic individual needs to think more rationally, and so forth. Tools such as psychoactive medication or intensive remediation programs can help achieve these aims.

6. **Success in Life Also Depends on Modifying Your Surrounding Environment to Fit the Needs of Your Unique Brain (Niche Construction)**. We shouldn't focus all of our attention on making a neurodiverse person adapt to the environment in which they find themselves, which is a little like making a round peg fit in a square hole. We should also devise ways of helping an individual change their surrounding environment to fit the needs of their unique brain.

7. **Niche Construction Includes Career and Lifestyle Choices, Assistive Technologies, Human Resources, and Other Life-Enhancing Strategies Tailored to the Specific Needs of a Neurodiverse Individual.** There are many tools, resources, and strategies for altering the environment so that it meshes with the needs of a neurodiverse brain. For example, a person with ADHD can find a career that involves novelty and movement, use an iPhone to help with organizing his day, and hire a coach to assist him with developing better social skills.

8. **Positive Niche Construction Directly Modifies the Brain, Which in Turn Enhances its Ability to Adapt to the Environment.** In experiments with mice, neuroscientists have shown that a more enriching environment results in a more complex network of neuronal connections in the brain. This more complex brain, in turn, has an easier time adapting to the needs of the surrounding environment. (Armstrong, n.d., para. 5)

In defense of his view that neurodiversity should be seen as an asset rather than a defect, Armstrong points out that countless neurodiverse people not only lead highly productive lives, but they also perform with excellence on tasks well matched to their modes of brain functioning.

THE POWER OF "THINKING DIFFERENT"

In the words of William Arthur Ward, "Teaching is more than imparting knowledge; it is inspiring change. Learning is more than absorbing facts; it is acquiring understanding." Educators play a foundational role in shaping society's perceptions of countless aspects of life, including perspectives regarding neurodiversity. In a neurodiverse world, teachers in many cases exercise tremendous leverage in spreading wider appreciation of the power of neurodiversity and empowering students who think differently to meaningfully impact mainstream thought, culture, and life.

The power and possibilities inherent in celebrating neurodiversity and appreciating the value of thinking differently were famously highlighted in a classic commercial by Apple Inc. (1997). In their "Think Different" campaign's *Crazy Ones* commercial, the following words were combined with inspirational music and video clips of noteworthy difference-makers throughout history, including Albert Einstein, Thomas Edison, Muhammad Ali, Mahatma Gandhi, Amelia Earhart, and Martin Luther King Jr.:

Here's to the crazy ones.
The misfits.
The rebels.
The troublemakers.
The round pegs in the square holes.
The ones who see things differently.
They're not fond of rules.
And they have no respect for the status quo.
You can quote them, disagree with them, glorify, or vilify them.
About the only thing you can't do is ignore them.
Because they change things.
They invent.
They imagine.
They heal.
They explore.
They create.
They inspire.
They push the human race forward.
Maybe they have to be crazy.
How else can you stare at an empty canvas and see a work of art?

Or sit in silence and hear a song that's never been
written?
Or gaze at a red planet and see a laboratory on wheels?
We make tools for these kinds of people.
While some see them as the crazy ones, we see genius.
Because the people who are crazy enough to think they
can change the world, are the ones who do.

Although the version of the commercial narrated by actor
Richard Dreyfuss ultimately aired on television, another version
was narrated by co-founder, chairman, and CEO of Apple Inc.,
Steve Jobs. In fact, on the morning of the first date the commercial was scheduled to air, Jobs ultimately decided to select the
version narrated by Dreyfuss; in his view, the "Think Different"
campaign was about Apple Inc. and not about Jobs himself.

In the now famous campaign's development stages, Jobs
insisted that instead of the campaign being called "Think Differently," the word "different" be utilized as a noun, such as in the
phrases "think big" or "think beauty." Upon its release, the "Think
Different" campaign became a tremendous hit. Widely celebrated,
the *Crazy Ones* commercial earned many significant accolades and
awards, including the 1998 Emmy Award for Best Commercial
and the 2000 Grand Effie Award for most effective campaign in
America.

The campaign garnered extensive attention and appeal for
many reasons, including the powerful emotions it conveyed and
its memorable inspirational qualities. The video clips displayed
throughout the commercial feature many individuals who were
criticized throughout their lives for thinking differently, yet each
of them ultimately made profound positive impacts upon the
world and left lasting legacies behind, long after their passing.

The commercial brought to light and celebrated the power of
thinking differently, feeling differently, and behaving differently.
It honored those "round pegs" who cannot be made to fit within

"square holes." Ultimately, these individuals often turn out to be so much more than different thinkers. In fact, those different thinkers frequently become difference makers.

THE RIPPLE EFFECTS OF NEURODIVERSITY IN THE CLASSROOM

The "unique" kindergartener, sixth grader, or high school sophomore in any given classroom may not likely appear to be the brilliant engineer, author, or entrepreneur they will eventually become. In many educational settings, recognizing such potential poses a significant challenge for today's educators. As they seek to effectively support dozens of learners, all facing unique needs, teachers may experience difficulty fully recognizing each student's unique giftings.

Even still, when a teacher notices a student's potential—even hidden potential—they support that student in taking steps toward becoming their best selves. However, it is important to note that challenges related to teaching neurodiverse learners do not instantaneously disappear as educators recognize the benefits of neurodiversity.

Rentenbach, Prislovsky, and Gabriel (2017) offer practical suggestions for appreciating and even celebrating neurodiversity (specifically autism, ADHD, and dyslexia) while supporting diverse learners in meeting their highest potential. These suggestions are overviewed in the coming sections.

PRACTICAL IMPLICATIONS FOR SUPPORTING STUDENTS WITH AUTISM

1. *Presume competence even when you don't see or hear it yet.* Teachers should avoid assuming intellectual disability on the basis of unique behaviors or difficulty in communication. So much can be accomplished through treating others with respect. Learners should be gifted the freedom to consistently rise to expectations—and surpassing these

expectations may ultimately follow. Educators should also avoid assuming that students with autism do not have the ability to hear or understand verbal communication. They may hear far more than teachers realize, allowing them to begin to develop assumptions regarding which adults can be trusted. This also provides students with cues about whether those adults who discuss their behaviors and abilities actually believe in them. Respect in communication is key.

2. *Smile.* Students with autism often sense and take on the feelings of those surrounding them. Others who demonstrate joy, confidence, sincerity, and positive energy support these students in finding new tasks more appealing. When adults express that they are burned-out, apathetic, dishonest, or cynical in the presence of students with autism, they can have detrimental impacts upon learners' growth and development.

3. *Listen.* When supporting nonverbal students with autism, listening may not seem helpful or necessary. Even still, the act of listening involves an effort to hear, to notice, and to heed. When these students are not typing or talking, teachers should find alternative ways to observe and to listen. Educators should seek to learn about their past, their interests, and the things in life that bring them joy. After discovering at least one of their interests, teachers can leverage this as a means of opening doors to new learning experiences and new opportunities for socialization. As when working with any learner, familiar themes and favorite passions bring about new chances to initiate the development of academic and social skills that may not come as easily for students with autism.

4. *Wait.* What students with autism may view as stillness, others may view as wasting time. Yet learners with autism often

appreciate the realities of impermanence. Embracing time to process and to think represents an important component of their daily routines. This process may not fit within the structure of more traditional learning environments in which learners must create written responses immediately after completing a reading assignment. Even still, the act of providing downtime to ponder a plan for responding during the school day or even overnight might be exactly what is needed to bring about fresh insights. The act of providing "think time" benefits not only students with autism, but it also proves helpful for a wide variety of learners.

5. *Make room for nonverbal communication.* For students with autism, verbal language may prove an uncomfortable way to communicate. Even still, their thinking is not "faulty"—it may simply not be based in language. For some, typing may make communication easier, as the speed of each thought is controlled and can be divided into smaller components.

PRACTICAL IMPLICATIONS FOR SUPPORTING STUDENTS WITH ADHD

Weiss (2005), a psychologist, wrote a list of "29 positive attributes of ADD" (using the term "ADD" to include ADD as well as ADHD). This list began with traits such as sensitive and empathetic and concluded with observant, loyal, and wholehearted. Recognizing positive traits and creating classrooms in which these traits are cultivated represent two entirely different endeavors. The following list, also compiled by Rentenbach, Prislovsky, and Gabriel (2017), overviews practical suggestions for effectively supporting students with ADHD:

1. *Let students know that human excellence comes in all packages—so they are invited to be themselves.* When teachers cannot identify students' key strengths, watching and asking

questions typically proves to be very helpful. Although learners may not be able to articulate their individual strengths, observing students' processes of pursuing interests and passions is an excellent starting point. Discovering places in which ADHD students feel capable and comfortable offers a helpful foundation for trust and connection. For example, asking ADHD students about the portion of their day that brings them the most joy or offers them a sense of calm may support this process. Each week, teachers should endeavor to provide at least one chance to learn, collaborate, and communicate in a way that targets their strengths.

2. *Don't make unrealistic restrictions on movement.* Learners with ADHD may feel most comfortable when they have opportunities to be active. Instead of mandating that students remain still, teachers can support ADHD students through providing key moments for movement. For example, Rentenbach, Prislovsky, and Gabriel (2017) suggest that when giving partner-based assignments, educators offer students the opportunity to walk around the room as they discuss ideas. Throughout class discussions, students might be given the chance to sit in rocking chairs or on exercise balls. During review assignments, learners could be invited to toss a ball to one another in the classroom.

3. *Create some routines.* For students with ADHD, as with many learners, predictable structures represent a key component of learning. Class routines may help students develop patterns of thinking and performing more effectively. Though devoting regular timeframes for certain activities, teachers provide the chance for students to plan their attention as well as to focus on one item to be accomplished at a time.

4. *Understand that people with ADHD are drawn to intense stimuli—and go for it.* Within the human brain, the chemical

dopamine relates to motivation, reward seeking, and movement. This often results in people with ADHD seeking increased stimulation and even extreme thrills. It is for this reason that individuals with ADHD comprise a large percentage of athletes, explorers, and entrepreneurs. Students with ADHD thrive when provided opportunities to help with movement-oriented portions of lessons. For example, delivering messages between groups, reorganizing spaces devoted to classroom activities, and handing out materials provide excellent opportunities for ADHD students to engage with the class in meaningful ways involving movement. Rewarding them for excellent work might include opportunities for stimulation, such as increased recess time. Some students may even thrive through added physical challenges to their daily activities, such as balancing on one foot as they read a text or respond to questions.

5. *Be patient with yourself as you learn more and do better.* As teachers demonstrate their willingness to take risks and to learn from mistakes, this encourages learners to do likewise.

PRACTICAL IMPLICATIONS FOR SUPPORTING STUDENTS WITH DYSLEXIA

As a result of a different brain organization pattern, the dyslexic brain is not efficiently wired for spelling and word recognition. However, there are also considerable advantages to this neurological organization. The Eides (2012), two leading learning sciences scholars, identified four discrete talents providing key benefits for individuals with dyslexia. They developed the acronym MIND to encompass advanced skills in material reasoning, interconnected reasoning, narrative/story-based reasoning, and dynamic reasoning.

This provides an encouraging perspective regarding the abilities of individuals with dyslexia, especially because these abilities impact literacy skills including comprehension, the process of making meaning, the act of drawing inferences, and the skill of making connections between ideas. Although the dyslexic brain may find foundational skills such as spelling and word recognition challenging, it seems especially suited to effectively engage in more advanced literacy-related activities.

While the Eides (2012) acknowledge that those with dyslexia may encounter certain impairments, challenges, and frustrations within academic contexts, they advocate for looking beyond such difficulties and recognizing that dyslexia encompasses far more than reading challenges. In fact, dyslexia represents a systematic form of language processing that carries certain key advantages.

Although people with dyslexia vary in countless ways, they are statistically more apt to possess essential skills that support them in effectively navigating within a variety of career fields. For example, their ability to grasp a broader vision and avoid the pitfalls of getting lost in details serves to support many people with dyslexia in thriving in corporate settings. By embracing such skills within classrooms contexts, these skills can be leveraged as sources of strength for dyslexic learners.

1. *Make print worth it.* Considering that it will take additional time, skill, effort, and courage for certain learners to consume text-based materials without support, teachers encourage and motivate dyslexic learners by creating purposes for reading that compel students and associate with their interests and goals. For instance, a student interested in the culinary arts might be more motivated to read a text regarding cooking skills than other texts unrelated to their interests.

2. *Accommodate now.* Students learning to navigate print-based learning activities that necessitate reading and writing still need and desire access to important content, seek out chances to participate in learning, and appreciate opportunities to

leverage their strengths. Teachers can do this by providing audiobooks and/or videos, as well as through giving students the chance to convey their learning using oral and visual presentations. Dyslexic students may require consistent effort and extended time to develop key literacy strategies and skills. As they do this, communication and comprehension building should not be paused. By providing dyslexic learners with engaging, meaningful texts, crucial content can be conveyed in a variety of ways.

3. *Invest in strategies that work.* Typically, students can determine whether a remedial program or intervention strategy is effectively supporting them, even before anyone else. Because the processes of developing writing, spelling, and reading skills might require extended time and effort, this instruction should effectively empower students to leverage their strengths and achieve visible progress.

4. *Communicate the strengths as well as the patterns of difficulty that dyslexia signifies.* Teachers should intentionally incorporate instructional strategies so that students with disability labels, as well as their classmates, understand and appreciate the power of neurodiversity, particularly within opportunities for teamwork. This may help to negate the shame and isolation that students struggling to read may otherwise encounter.

5. *Cultivate the advantages of dyslexia.* If students must consistently progress through independent reading assignments prior to engaging in activities in class, they may not be able to fully participate with classmates. Teachers can avoid this dilemma by providing roles within smaller groups and implementing activities that build upon creativity and reasoning instead of the processing of texts as a prerequisite for participation. This might include asking dyslexic learners to

engage through responsibilities that include problem solving and participation rather than requiring them to read aloud or serve as scribes.

Little by little, seemingly typical moments within daily classroom interactions mold students' perceptions regarding learning, school, others, and themselves. The above implications shared by Rentenbach, Prislovsky, and Gabriel (2017) serve as a starting point for conversations and reflections that extend as more individuals learn of and share the advantages of neurodiversity within classroom settings and beyond.

QUESTIONS FOR REFLECTION

Each day contains exactly 24 hours—that's 1,440 minutes. A relatively small investment of 15 to 30 minutes per day devoted to deeply, genuinely reflecting on the following questions will undoubtedly reap long-lasting dividends. Heartfelt reflection fuels the journey toward developing a learning community built on strengths, positively impacting the lives of countless students. The more honest each answer, the greater the potential impact. Now is the time to celebrate our differences!

- Of Armstrong's (2011) eight principles of neurodiversity (below), which most surprised or stood out to you, and why?

  1. The Human Brain Works More Like an Ecosystem than a Machine.

  2. Human Brains Exist Along Continuums of Competence.

  3. Human Competence is Defined by the Values of the Culture to Which You Belong.

  4. Whether You are Regarded as Disabled or Gifted Depends Largely on When and Where You Were Born.

5. Success in Life is Based on Adapting One's Brain to the Needs of the Surrounding Environment.

6. Success in Life Also Depends on Modifying Your Surrounding Environment to Fit the Needs of Your Unique Brain (Niche Construction).

7. Niche Construction Includes Career and Lifestyle Choices, Assistive Technologies, Human Resources, and Other Life-Enhancing Strategies Tailored to the Specific Needs of a Neurodiverse Individual.

8. Positive Niche Construction Directly Modifies the Brain, Which in Turn Enhances its Ability to Adapt to the Environment.

- Have you ever viewed Apple Inc.'s *Crazy Ones* commercial? If so, how did it make you feel? What characteristics did the individuals you recognized in the commercial have in common? How might the world have been different without their lives and legacies?

- Of the practical suggestions offered for supporting students with autism, ADHD, and dyslexia, did you come across any that would also be helpful for supporting students who do not have autism, ADHD, and dyslexia? Which suggestions might be most helpful? Why?

ESSENTIAL IDEAS TO REMEMBER

Rather than being seen as challenging, students with "differently wired" brains should be viewed as "neurodiverse." It is also vital for educators to help neurodiverse learners consider how their neurodiversity empowers them to excel in areas that might not otherwise be possible. Ultimately, neurodiversity should be viewed as an asset instead of a deficit.

Educators play a key role in influencing society's viewpoints on many aspects of life, including perspectives regarding neurodiversity. In a neurodiverse world, teachers often hold great capacity to spread wider appreciation for the benefits of neurodiversity. Their influence may even serve to empower students who think differently to profoundly impact mainstream thought, culture, and life.

The following chapters offer practical applications for supporting every student with skills for future success in life, as well as the inspiration needed to ultimately change the world, one life at a time. Because, in the words of Steve Jobs, "The people who are crazy enough to think they can change the world, are the ones who do."

REFERENCES

Apple Inc. (1997). *Crazy ones* [television commercial]. Los Angeles, CA: TBWA\Chiat\Day.

Armstrong, T. (2011). *The Power of neurodiversity: Unleashing the advantages of your differently wired brain* (published in hardcover as *Neurodiversity*). New York: Da Capo Press.

Armstrong, T. (n.d.). Neurodiversity: A concept whose time has come. American Institute for Learning and Development. https://www.institute4learning.com/resources/articles/neurodiversity/.

Baker, D. (2011). *The politics of neurodiversity: Why public policy matters.* Boulder, CO: Lynne Rienner.

Eide, B. & Eide, F. (2012). *The dyslexic advantage: Unlocking the hidden potential of the dyslexic brain.* New York: Plume.

Gilger, J., & Kaplan, B. (2001). Atypical brain development: A conceptual framework for understanding developmental learning disabilities. *Developmental Neuropsychology 20*(2): 465–81.

Griffiths, D. (2020) Teaching for neurodiversity: Training teachers to see beyond labels. *Impact Journal of Chartered College of Teaching* (8).

Jones, A., & Kindersley, K. (2013). Dyslexia: Assessing and reporting. *The PATOSS Guide*, 2nd ed. London: Hodder Education.

Lewis, A., & Norwich, B. (2004). Overview and discussion: Overall conclusions. In: Lewis, A. and Norwich, B. (Eds.) *Special Teaching for Special Children? Pedagogies for Inclusion.* Buckingham: Open University Press, pp. 206–23.

Rentenbach, B., Prislovsky, L., & Gabriel, R. (2017). Valuing differences: Neurodiversity in the classroom. *Phi Delta Kappan, 98*(8), 59–63.

Singer, J. (1999). "Why can't you be normal for once in your life?" From a "problem with no name" to the emergence of a new category of difference.

In: Corker, M. and French, S. (Eds.) *Disability Discourse*. Buckingham/Philadelphia: Open University Press, pp. 59– 67.

Weiss, L. (2005). *Attention deficit disorder in adults: A different way of thinking*. Boulder: CO: Taylor Trade Publishing.

CHAPTER 4

Capitalizing on Collaboration

Teamwork Makes the Dream Work

Alone we can do so little; together we can do so much.
—HELEN KELLER

KING SOLOMON OF ISRAEL, THE BENEFICIARY OF UNPARALLELED wisdom, famously remarked, "Two are better than one, because they have a good return for their labor: if either of them falls down, one can help the other up. But pity anyone who falls and has no one to help them up" (*New International Version*, 2011, Ecclesiastes 4:9–10). This wise principle applies to countless aspects of life, including educational settings.

In a world in which individualism is prized and teachers often work in silos, far too many educators overlook the power of connectivity. This chapter presents practical steps for discovering, developing, and capitalizing upon "perfect pairings" to cultivate student success, including partnerships with fellow teachers and administrators.

Functional tools for building capacity to collaborate with a community of learners who will make a strengths-based teaching paradigm happen are within reach. Strengths-based teaching and learning allow teachers and students to collaborate and add value to the learning experience for all. Once people learn to capitalize on strengths together, the magic of transformed educational experiences truly happens.

THE INEVITABILITY OF INCREASING ISOLATION—AND HOW TO STOP IT!

Far too often, individuals within today's educational settings work in isolation. Yet this phenomenon is not limited to academic contexts. The book *The Maximizer Mindset: Work Less, Achieve More, Spread Joy* (Alaniz & Hao, 2021) offers the following glimpse into the inevitability of increasing isolation within today's word:

> While individualism is believed to be increasing among Western cultures, research also suggests that the perception of individualism may be rising around the world. In fact, heightened socioeconomic expansion is a particularly powerful predictor of more common individualistic behaviors and values within a country over time. (Santos, Varnum, & Grossmann, 2017, p. 64)

In the words of Henri Santos of the University of Waterloo,

> Much of the research on the manifestation of rising individualism—showing, for example, increasing narcissism and higher divorce rates—has focused on the United States. Our findings show that this pattern also applies to other countries that are not Western or industrialized. . . . Although there are still cross-national differences in individualism-collectivism, the data indicate that, overall, most countries are moving towards greater individualism. (Santos & Grossmann, 2017, para. 2)

According to Alaniz and Hao (2021),

> As more and more cultures idolize productivity, the value of relationships is increasingly becoming a secondary, tertiary, or even lesser consideration. In a world in which "looking out

for number one" is often encouraged—even if at times not overtly—other people's needs may be considered nothing more than an inconvenience. When production is placed before people and individualism is idolized, we face the danger of missing out on "the stuff of life." . . . Solid relationships comprise an essential component of a healthy life, according to research that demonstrates that strong connections with others elongate our lives, enable us to more effectively handle stress, and encourage us to develop healthier daily habits. . . . An existence without relationships is actually as unhealthy as smoking when it comes to life expectancy (Holt-Lunstad, Smith, & Layton, 2010). As social beings, our relationships impact our health mentally, emotionally, and physically. The quality of the relationships we maintain is the greatest predictor of our quality of life—greater than financial success, wealth, fame, or status. (pp. 65–66)

Quality relationships comprise a necessary aspect of every area of life, including academic settings. A brief published by Ed Trust and MDRC (2021) highlights the importance of strong relationships in schools, especially in light of the impacts of the COVID-19 pandemic. According to the brief,

Educators are facing their own personal stresses, in addition to being concerned about teaching academic content and about the well-being of their students, which can ultimately wear on their well-being. But even with all of these stressors, teachers and students are trying to remain connected to schools and each other. Strong relationships with teachers and school staff can dramatically enhance students' level of motivation and therefore promote learning. (p. 2)

In fact, when learners can access strong relationships within school settings and beyond, they are often more engaged in academic pursuits, exhibit greater social skills, and display positive behaviors more frequently (Roehlkepartain et al., 2017). Unfortunately, in today's world, too few students encounter this type of experience.

A recent survey of 25,400 sixth through twelfth graders within a highly diverse, large school district discovered that fewer than one-third of the middle school participants cultivated strong relationships with teachers, and this number fell to 16 percent by their senior year of high school (Roehlkepartain et al., 2017). Additionally, learners of lower-income socioeconomic statuses indicate that they maintain even fewer strong relationships among teachers (Scales et al., 2020).

The Ed Trust and MDRC (2021) brief also offers the following chart overviewing foundational elements of building strong relationships within school settings (and beyond), as well as sample actions for each element and explanations of how these actions can be displayed.

ESSENTIAL QUESTIONS FOR TEACHERS AND SCHOOL LEADERS TO CONSIDER

Ed Trust and MDRC's brief (2021) also overviews key questions for educational leaders to consider, including the following:

Who benefits most from strong relationships?
Students who experience either a high level of environmental adversity or a high level of personal challenge (i.e., academic or behavioral) benefit the most.

Why are strong relationships important?
Strong relationships provide a foundation for student engagement, belonging, and, ultimately, learning. The more high-quality relationships students have with their teachers, the better their engagement in school.

How can schools strengthen relationships among students and staff?
The most important thing schools can do to foster these relationships is to have a culture that explicitly values adults nurturing relationships with students and providing teachers and school staff with the time, space, and occasions to interact repeatedly with individual students, especially those that seem less engaged.

Table 4.1

Building Developmental Relationships	
Elements	Sample Actions (and Explanations)
Express Care	Be dependable (someone I can trust)
	Listen (really pay attention)
	Encourage (praise my efforts and achievements)
	Believe in me (make me feel known and valued)
Challenge Growth	Expect my best (expect me to live up to my potential)
	Hold me accountable (insist I take responsibility for my actions)
	Help me reflect on failures (help me learn from my mistakes)
	Stretch me (push me to go further)
Provide Support	Navigate (guide me through hard situations)
	Empower me (build my confidence to take charge of my life)
	Advocate (defend me when I need it)
	Set boundaries (establish limits to keep me on track)
Share Power	Respect me (take me seriously and treat me fairly)
	Include me (involve me in decisions that affect me)
	Collaborate (work with me to solve problems and reach goals)
	Let me lead (create opportunities for me to take action)
Expand Responsibilities	Inspire (inspire me to see possibilities for my future)
	Broaden horizons (expose me to new experiences, ideas, and places)
	Connect (introduce me to more people who can help me)

NOTE: THIS TABLE IS ADAPTED FROM THE WORK OF ROEHLKEPARTAIN ET AL. (2017) AND FEATURED IN ED TRUST AND MDRC (2021).

- Start informally with teachers and staff, taking time to get to know individual students and consistently checking in. Once trust is established, the relationship will grow.
- Formalize interactions between students and staff in scheduled activities to ensure they happen.
- Have adults meet one-on-one or in small groups with students, and have activity driven by students' goals and desires.

Which adult relationships are most impactful?

All in-school adults should strive for strong relationships with students. When students have strong relationships with their teachers, in-class motivation increases the most. In these instances, students are motivated by teachers' high expectations as well as their own. (pp. 4–5)

BECOMING A PERSON OF INFLUENCE (WITHIN SCHOOL SETTINGS AND BEYOND)

While countless individuals within and outside of educational contexts spend the majority of their days working in siloed isolation, simple and easily implemented strategies serve to open doors of communication and partnership.

The classic book *How to Win Friends and Influence People* (Carnegie, 1964) offers timeless principles for capitalizing on the power of collaboration. Author Dale Carnegie, a former salesman, experienced such great success in sales within his territory that he was promoted to the national leader for his firm. Eventually, Carnegie transitioned from sales to teaching others about public speaking, earning $500 per week—equivalent to nearly $11,800 today. In fact, notable individuals like Warren Buffet participated in Carnegie's courses.

Carnegie's principles regarding the power of prioritizing people were encapsulated in his book. The following represent several principles for cultivating supportive, collaborative relationships:

1. *Don't criticize, condemn, or complain.* Psychologist B. F. Skinner's now famous research studies revealed that as animals receive rewards for positive behaviors, they learn more efficiently and retain more effectively than after receiving punishment for negative behavior. Skinner's studies have been followed by additional research indicating that this same concept also applies to human behavior. Criticism does not produce positive results and will never lead to lasting change. Ultimately, criticism leads to resentment. Pride and ego often motivate people, who are creatures of emotion and not logic.

2. *Give honest and sincere appreciation.* Although most of the key desires people crave (e.g., the desire for food, sleep, money, etc.) are typically or ultimately satisfied, one yearning—almost as deeply rooted as the yearning for food or sleep—is not met as often. Namely, the desire to be viewed as important is not as frequently attained in many people's lives. Unfortunately, almost by default, people take other people for granted. Yet, earnest and deliberate words of encouragement hold the power to alter people's perspectives of themselves, increase their motivation, and boost their success. Sincere words of affirmation cost nothing and hold the potential to considerably enhance the lives of others.

3. *Arouse in other people an eager want.* Lloyd George, the prime minister of Great Britain during World War I, maintained a position of power for years after other wartime leaders. When asked to offer strategies for his success over the years, his response was simple but profound. He uncovered the importance of a key principle: "Bait the hook to suit the fish." Basically, it is important to offer others what they value and desire rather than what the person offering values and desires.

This principle greatly enhances the possibilities of impacting others, as opportunities are framed in terms of people's motivations. This is impossible without empathy. Upon seeking to view another's situation from their perspective rather than making assumptions, baiting the hook to suit the fish becomes far more feasible.

By default, many people spend their entire lives without taking time or devoting the effort to view situations from other's perspectives. Yet, when long-held viewpoints and desires are set aside to make room for new perspectives, the possibilities of persuading others to collaborate in accomplishing important goals greatly broaden. Those who seek to serve others without selfish motivations hold countless advantages over the majority who devote their days to looking out for their own interests. In the words of Carnegie, "You can make more friends in two months by becoming interested in other people than you can in two years by trying to get other people interested in you."

Although Carnegie did not intend for the principles within his book to be utilized exclusively in school settings, they powerfully impact the foundational relationships needed to build a strengths-based culture of student success. Whether in interactions between students or faculty and staff, the sky is the limit in cultivating a culture focusing on strengths when these simple, yet profound, strategies are applied.

As today's teachers and administrators reflect on their past schooling experiences, they may unfortunately remember situations in which criticizing, condemning, and complaining seemed the norm. Memories of teachers, staff members, school leaders, or parents making disparaging remarks regarding their performance in school may negatively impact a students' views regarding how positive, safe, and encouraging schools can be for learners.

Most individuals can remember a harsh or condemning statement made by someone within their developmental years; for many, such memories are not soon forgotten and may easily leave scars for years and years to come. These scars might later emerge as deeply embedded insecurities, an overwhelming fear of failure, or even a complete unwillingness to try again.

Some faculty and staff within today's school settings intentionally pursue careers in education as a means of combatting this type of disparaging behavior. They serve students because they want to make a difference through identifying and building on students' strengths. They may have faced criticism, condemnation, or complaining as they progressed through their developmental years and want to now provide a vastly different experience for their own students.

On the other hand, some faculty and staff naturally default to criticism, condemnation, or complaining—whether in the presence of students or colleagues—because this is the example that was set for them throughout their schooling years. Their scars from past hurts seem to thrust them into repeated patterns of discouraging behaviors, and it can be difficult to overcome years and years of unresolved pain. In such situations, there is obviously a better way; yet it can be challenging to know where to begin.

Talli Goldman-Dolge (2021), CEO of the Mobile Mental Wellness Collaborative and senior vice president of School and Community Partnerships for Meadows Mental Health Policy Institute, offers ten practical suggestions for developing positive perspectives and behaviors within a negative world:

1. Limit exposure to media and social media.
   Overconsumption of social media and news surrounding the pandemic has led to more mental health challenges. Instead of randomly consuming social media and news throughout the day, consider blocking off a part of your day for it, such as 30 minutes in the morning and 30 minutes in the evening.

2. Reframe your thoughts.

   When we are defeated, it is easy to think negatively. A lot of times those automatic thoughts aren't true and should be replaced with a more balanced thought. For example, some people are struggling financially these days. They might be thinking "I'm so irresponsible. I'm never going to climb out of this hole." Instead, they could say "When I look at all my debt, I am overwhelmed. But there are small actions I can take now to start getting out of debt."

3. Use a mantra.

   Having prepared statements to say to yourself can help you silence the negative voices in your head. Some examples include "You can do hard things" or "It is going to be okay." What is your mantra? Pick one that fits you and say it to yourself often so that when negative thoughts sneak in your head, your mantra is right there to pull you through.

4. Find your passion.

   Find something that brings you joy and then make time for it. Maybe there's something you used to do that made you happy that has dropped out of your routine. Is it exercising, watching the sunset, drawing, or something else? Putting it back into your life, or adding something new, in a small dose can exponentially change the way you view your own happiness.

5. Listen to music.

   Uplifting music is a powerful tool to boost your mood, as your body releases dopamine, the feel-good hormone. I personally love finding music I haven't heard in a long time that brings up a positive memory. It's beautiful to revisit the positive feelings I had during the period of time that the music reminds me of.

6. Surround yourself with positive people.

   Even positive people can struggle with negativity if they are surrounded by scared and anxious people. Make sure to include people in your life who can find the good during this challenging time.

7. Do something nice for someone.

   Get out of your head by helping someone. When you do a good deed for someone else, it not only improves the mood of the person you helped, but it also improves your mood AND the mood of anyone who witnessed the good deed. A great way to experience this is by volunteering.

8. Make a list.

   Write down the things you are most proud about yourself. Put that list in a well-trafficked part of your home so that you can read it daily. I want you to read it so often that it becomes a natural thing for you to talk about with loved ones.

9. Write a letter.

   Pick up a pen and paper and handwrite a letter of gratitude to someone you appreciate. Be sure to share with them what you think makes them special. This act will show you the depth of human kindness and the way it contributes to your own happiness.

10. Go outside.

    Now is a great time to be outside in nature, taking in the changing seasons. . . . Life isn't just about what you experience today. (Goldman-Dolge, 2021, paras. 6–15)

Dr. Barbara Fredrickson (2009), positivity researcher at the University of North Carolina, discovered that for every negative, heart-wrenching emotional experience endured, human beings must in turn experience at least three positive, heartfelt emotional experiences to feel uplifted. Applying the "3-to-1 ratio," a term coined by Frederickson, cultivates a collaborative relationship between efforts to survive versus efforts to thrive. According to Frederickson, positivity is far more than a "grin and bear it" mentality. It encompasses an entire range of emotions to overcome negativity, from amusement to joy, appreciation to love, hope to gratitude, and more.

As an example of the power of negative thinking to impact human memory, most Americans of a certain age can easily recall exactly where they were and what they were doing when they first learned of the horrific events that unfolded on September 11, 2001. They likely remember the first person they called or interacted with as soon as they learned of the initial airplane striking the World Trade Center. Yet they may not remember the exact circumstances of their lives even a day prior to that fateful September 11.

This is because negative emotional experiences indelibly impact human beings in ways that other experiences do not, and this applies to learners as well—whether young or old. Those who serve students within school settings wield a "superpower" of sorts—the power to forever change the trajectory of students' lives through positive words of encouragement. While most adults can readily recall a teacher who caused emotional scarring through negative communication, many also fondly remember a teacher or mentor who empowered them to soar in one or more areas of life through their consistent, intentional, uplifting communication.

Each day, faculty and staff within school settings hold the power to decide which type of educator they will be for the students under their influence. As Carnegie (1964) famously shared, honest, sincere appreciation and empathy carry others farther in life than one can possibly imagine. This is especially true in school settings, in which learners face among the most pivotal years of their lives. A kind, caring educator with heartfelt appreciation for students' strengths holds the potential to empower students to accomplish more in school—and more beyond their schooling years—than they ever imagined possible.

Questions for Reflection

Each day contains exactly 24 hours—that's 1,440 minutes. A relatively small investment of 15 to 30 minutes per day devoted to deeply, genuinely reflecting on the following questions will undoubtedly reap long-lasting dividends. Heartfelt reflection fuels the journey toward developing a learning community built on strengths, positively impacting the lives of countless students. The more honest each answer, the greater the potential impact. Now is the time to capitalize on collaboration!

- On a scale from 1 to 10, with 10 being the highest rating, take a moment to rate how positive you feel about your relationships with your colleagues. How satisfied are you with this number?

- Do you wish this number was higher? If so, think of three relationships you would like to be stronger and list them.

- For each of the relationships you listed, reflect on one next step you can take to intentionally invest in this person's life. Write your action plan, including a timeline for fulfilling this plan.

- As you interact with students, which of the following principles (Carnegie, 1964) seems most challenging? Why do you believe this to be the case?
  - Don't criticize, condemn, or complain.
  - Give honest and sincere appreciation.
  - Arouse in people a want.

- Are you able to remember a teacher throughout your schooling years who consistently and effectively demonstrated the principle that seems most difficult now? What strategies did this teacher use to positively influence your life?

- Don't criticize, condemn, or complain.
- Give honest and sincere appreciation.
- Arouse in people a want.

- Of the strategies you shared above, which one could you intentionally begin integrating in your interactions with students?
- Which three students will you exercise these strategies with over the coming weeks?

ESSENTIAL IDEAS TO REMEMBER

Charles Schwab once remarked, "I have yet to find the man, however exalted his station, who did not do better work and put forth greater effort under a spirit of approval than under a spirit of criticism." Positive relational investment is the fuel that propels students' confidence, and ultimately, their achievement. When faculty and staff partner with students and one another in meaningful ways, the sky is the limit.

Through developing strategies to replace the temptation to criticize, condemn, or complain with positive thinking—whether communicating with learners or colleagues—educators pave the way for student success. By sharing honest and sincere appreciation for students' characteristics and the work they produce, the adults within their lives support them in overcoming setbacks and striving for new milestones. Through educators' efforts to empathize with learners, seeking to treat them as they would have wanted to be treated in school, students' growth, as well as their love for learning, are more apt to flourish now and well beyond their years in educational settings.

REFERENCES

Alaniz, K., & Hao, D. (2022). *The maximizer mindset: Work less, achieve more, spread joy*. Lanham, MD: Rowman & Littlefield Education.

Carnegie, D. (1964). *How to win friends and influence people*. New York: Simon and Schuster.

Ed Trust & MDRC. (2021). The importance of strong relationships: Strategies to solve unfinished learning. https://edtrust.org /wp-content/uploads/2021/03/Targeted-Intensive-Tutoring-as -a- Strategy-to-Solve-Unfinished-Learning-March-2021.pdf.

Fredrickson, B. L. (2009). *Positivity: Top-notch research reveals the 3-to-1 ration that will change your life*. New York: Three Rivers Press.

Goldman-Dolge, T. (2021, October). *10 ways to be positive in a negative world: How to combat negativity bias in your daily life*. KSAT.com. https: //www.ksat.com/news/local/2021/10/25/10-ways-to-be-positive-in-a -negative-world/.

Holt-Lunstad, J., Smith, T. B., & Layton, J. B. (2010). Social relationships and mortality risk: A meta-analytic review. *PLoS Medicine, 7*(7), e1000316. https://doi.org/10.1371/journal.pmed.1000316.

New International Version. (2011). BibleGateway.com. http://www.biblegateway .com/versions/New-International-Version-NIV-Bible/#booklist.

Roehlkepartain, E. C., Pekel, K., Syvertsen, A. K., Sethi, J., Sullivan, T. K., & Scales, P. C. (2017). *Relationships first: Creating connections that help young people thrive*. Minneapolis, MN: Search Institute, 1–20.

Santos, H. C, & Grossmann, I. (2017). *Individualistic practices and values increasing around the world*. Association for Psychological Sciences. https:// www.psychologicalscience.org/news/releases/individualistic-practices-and -values-increasing-around-the-world.html.

Santos, H. C., Varnum, M. E. W., & Grossmann, I. (2017). Global increases in individualism. *Psychological Science, 28*(9), 1228–39. https://doi.org/10 .1177/0956797617700622.

Scales, P.C., Van Boekel, M., Pekel, K., Syvertsen, A.K., & Roehlkepartain, E.C. (2020). Effects of developmental relationships with teachers on middle-school students' motivation and performance. *Psychology in the Schools, 57*(4), 646–77.

Tackling Technological Change

The Potential of Today's Innovative Educational Opportunities

Teachers need to integrate technology seamlessly into the curriculum instead of viewing it as an add-on, an afterthought, or an event.

—Heidi Hayes Jacobs

Students arrive at school with a variety of experiences and competencies; thus, simultaneously teaching twenty to thirty students (or more) with maximum effectiveness can present quite the challenge. This chapter focuses on how digital tools and resources in classroom environments allow for differentiated as well as reciprocal learning, as students learn alongside and from one another.

Teachers must make a wide range of decisions when considering student-centered technology integration. Today's digital tools and resources can ultimately provide greater accessibility for all learners, regardless of unique learning styles and differences. This chapter presents practical strategies for supporting learners in developing knowledge and skills for the digital age through purposeful technology integration.

In the book *Authentic Assessment in Action: An Everyday Guide for Bringing Learning to Life through Meaningful Assessment*, Alaniz and Cerling (2023) describe some of the promises (and pitfalls) of incorporating digital tools and resources within classroom settings:

> Digital innovation brings about many exciting promises within educational settings. Yet, unless educators grasp the WHY for integrating technology, these promises hold little value. Like most human beings, educators must discern the purpose of digital incorporation before they can embrace its advantages. Unless they perceive the association between technology integration and a sense of purpose, the opportunity for challenging learning endeavors, and the development of new meaning, they will likely not be motivated to incorporate digital tools and resources within their instructional endeavors. In the words of John Dewey, "If we teach today as we taught yesterday, we rob our children of tomorrow." In order for students to be prepared for the future, they must engage in innovative, future-focused learning endeavors today. Yet, this does not mean that educators should cram digital tools and resources into every lesson simply for the sake of ensuring that technology has been "integrated." In fact, student learning outcomes should drive technology integration and not vice versa. When educators feel pressured to incorporate digital tools and resources without clear purpose and intentional planning, these technologies may offer more harm than benefit. School districts and families would be wise to question the WHY for a given technology rather than focusing on integration for the sake of integration. (pp. 62–63)

Unless educators begin with the end in mind and focus upon the why when introducing and implementing instructional technologies, even the most innovative digital tools and resources will lack purpose and impact. Yet when technology is meaningfully integrated within classroom settings, the capacity for learners to grow and create in accordance with their strengths is greatly enhanced.

In this way, digital tools and resources hold the potential to play a vital role within strengths-based teaching and learning endeavors.

The TPACK Framework

In regard to the need for purpose when integrating technology in classroom settings, the TPACK framework (Herring, Koehler, & Mishra, 2016) fundamentally connects pedagogical strategies and content, interweaving them with the use of instructional technologies. TPACK focuses on the interrelatedness of the following types of knowledge: content knowledge (CK), pedagogical knowledge (PK), and technological knowledge (TK).

Rather than concentrating on these three aspects of teaching and learning independently, the TPACK framework accentuates the varieties of knowledge that occur within the intersections of these three forms of knowledge, namely pedagogical content knowledge (PCK), technological content knowledge (TCK), technological pedagogical knowledge (TPK), and technological pedagogical content knowledge (TPACK).

Regarding the importance of the TPACK model for today's learners, Alaniz (2021) states the following in *Collegial Coaching: Mentoring for Knowledge and Skills that Transfer to Real-world Applications*:

> Successful technology implementation requires effective pedagogical practices to convey essential content knowledge. . . . Individual students, unique teachers, differing developmental levels, shifting school settings, diverse demographics, and countless other factors guarantee that each circumstance will be unique. No one amalgamation of content, pedagogy, and technology will effectively serve students in every context. (p. 80)

The subsequent list offers a summary of these diverse knowledge types, constructed by Koehler (2012), one of the original designers of this classic educational framework:

- Content Knowledge (CK): "Teachers' knowledge about the subject matter to be learned or taught. The content to be covered in middle school science or history is different from the content to be covered in an undergraduate course on art appreciation or a graduate seminar on astrophysics. As Shulman (1986) noted, this knowledge would include knowledge of concepts, theories, ideas, organizational frameworks, knowledge of evidence and proof, as well as established practices and approaches toward developing such knowledge" (Koehler & Mishra, 2009).

- Pedagogical Knowledge (PK): "Teachers' deep knowledge about the processes and practices or methods of teaching and learning. They encompass, among other things, overall educational purposes, values, and aims. This generic form of knowledge applies to understanding how students learn, general classroom management skills, lesson planning, and student assessment" (Koehler & Mishra, 2009).

- Technology Knowledge (TK): "Knowledge about integrating technological tools and resources. This encompasses a broad enough understanding of technology that it can be applied in professional settings as well as in day-to-day life. This also entails recognition of when digital tools and resources can support or inhibit accomplishing set goals, as well as continued adaptation to as technological innovations occur" (Koehler & Mishra, 2009).

- Pedagogical Content Knowledge (PCK): "Consistent with and similar to Shulman's idea of knowledge of pedagogy that is applicable to the teaching of specific content. Central to Shulman's conceptualization of PCK is the notion of the transformation of the subject matter for teaching. Specifically, according to Shulman (1986), this transformation occurs as the teacher interprets the subject matter, finds multiple ways to represent it, and adapts and tailors the instructional materials to alternative conceptions and students' prior knowledge. PCK covers the core business of teaching, learning, curriculum, assessment, and reporting, such as the conditions that promote learning and the links among curriculum, assessment, and pedagogy" (Koehler & Mishra, 2009).

- Technological Content Knowledge (TCK): "An understanding of the manner in which technology and content influence and constrain one another. Teachers need to master more than the subject matter they teach; they must also have a deep understanding of the manner in which the subject matter (or the kinds of representations that can be constructed) can be changed by the application of particular technologies. Teachers need to understand which specific technologies are best suited for addressing subject-matter learning in their domains and how the content dictates or perhaps even changes the technology—or vice versa" (Koehler & Mishra, 2009).

- Technological Pedagogical Knowledge (TPK): "An understanding of how teaching and learning can change when particular technologies are used in particular ways. This includes knowing the pedagogical affordances and constraints of a range of technological tools as they relate to disciplinarily and developmentally appropriate pedagogical designs and strategies" (Koehler & Mishra, 2009).

- Technological Pedagogical Content Knowledge (TPACK): "Underlying truly meaningful and deeply skilled teaching with technology, TPACK is different from knowledge of all three concepts individually. Instead, TPACK is the basis of effective teaching with technology, requiring an understanding of the representation of concepts using technologies; pedagogical techniques that use technologies in constructive ways to teach content; knowledge of what makes concepts difficult or easy to learn and how technology can help redress some of the problems that students face; knowledge of students' prior knowledge and theories of epistemology; and knowledge of how technologies can be used to build on existing knowledge to develop new epistemologies or strengthen old ones" (Koehler & Mishra, 2009).

As instructional technologies are integrated with purpose and aligned with content knowledge and solid instructional strategies (as addressed by the TPACK framework), experiences involving the meaningful use of digital tools and resources within classroom settings abound. In fact, as stated by Alaniz (2021),

> Rather than merely sprinkling technology into instructional practices because it seems new or exciting, teachers must first develop a clear understanding of the goals and objectives upon which units and lessons will be built. . . . For example, technology may be employed by educators to augment instruction through video resources and presentations that deliver content through multiple modalities to support both auditory and visual learners. Technology provides teachers with strategies to demonstrate content through diverse media formats, including text, audio content, videos, hands-on modeling, and countless other applications. (p. 85)

THE FORMULA FOR AUTHENTIC LEARNING

As teachers plan and implement applicable, authentic learning opportunities, students gain meaningful academic experiences that translate beyond the walls of their classrooms to the world that awaits them in the future. Effective educators stimulate intrinsic motivation for learning through making learning applicable to the real world. Authentic learning opportunities revolutionize classroom contexts as students move from being passive information consumers to active co-creators of learning.

As shared by George Couros, a renowned educational speaker and teaching and leadership consultant, "Learning is creation, not consumption. Knowledge is not something a learner absorbs, but something a learner creates."

Alaniz (2021) presents a formula for authentic learning in *Collegial Coaching: Mentoring for Knowledge and Skills That Transfer to Real-World Applications*, which involves the facilitation of purposeful learning through instructional strategies grounded in applicability:

> [Teachers] do this by offering [students] real-world problems to solve, giving them opportunities to present solutions to various audiences, and designing assessment endeavors that apply to the everyday lives of learners. This method is summed up in an innovative formula for meaningful learning: authentic issues + authentic audiences + authentic assessment = authentic learning experiences. (p. 92)

Benjamin Disraeli, prime minister of the United Kingdom (1868 and 1874–1880), once stated, "The secret of success is constancy to purpose." Without purpose, planning and execution of learning endeavors lack meaning, and educators will find the task of inspiring students' motivation and passion for learning to be very difficult.

In the words of Alaniz and Cerling (2023),

> As educators introduce student learning outcomes and corresponding assessment endeavors to learners, the WHY must remain at the forefront. This inspires intrinsic motivation for learning, perseverance through academic challenges, and success in achieving student learning outcomes. The power of intrinsic motivation to impact student learning cannot be overstated. . . . Purpose is accomplished through aligning learning endeavors with real life, as students discern meaningful ways in which their experiences in the classroom translate to their

life beyond the walls of the classroom. As they recognize ties between the knowledge and skills inherent in learning outcomes and their current or future personal or professional experiences, they naturally become more invested in academic pursuits. . . . While today's educators may not know what future professional paths students will eventually take, they do have the opportunity to support them in gaining skills that will be necessary in any future professional context. (p. 50)

Fullan and Scott's (2014) previously examined white paper highlights the following novel instructional strategies for future-focused learning:

- Character: "Qualities of the individual essential for being personally effective in a complex world, including grit, tenacity, perseverance, resilience, reliability, and honesty."
- Citizenship: "Thinking like global citizens, considering global issues based on a deep understanding of diverse values with genuine interest in engaging with others to solve complex problems that impact human and environmental sustainability."
- Collaboration: "The capacity to work interdependently and synergistically in teams with strong interpersonal and team-related skills including effective management of team dynamics, making substantive decisions together, and learning from and contributing to the learning of others."
- Communication: "Mastery of three fluencies: digital, writing, and speaking tailored for a range of audiences."
- Creativity: "Having an 'entrepreneurial eye' for economic and social opportunities, asking the right questions to generate novel ideas, and demonstrating leadership to pursue those ideas into practice."

- Critical Thinking: "Critically evaluating information and arguments, seeing patterns and connections, construction meaningful knowledge and applying it in the real world." (pp. 6–7)

Authentic learning represents a foundational component of a strengths-based approach to education. Rather than focusing upon what students do not know, authentic learning endeavors allow students to build upon prior knowledge and skills to create new knowledge and skills. More traditional learning experiences often include a focus on preparing for upcoming quizzes and exams.

Yet, in the eyes of the learners themselves, quiz- and exam-based classroom activities may seem detached from life beyond the classroom. Rather than encouraging students to build upon the "Six Cs" of future-focused learning, a preoccupation with quizzes and exams encourages students to memorize material (often too much material to retain in the long term), only to forget the material as soon as the quiz or exam is over.

Quizzes and exams may also offer students with natural or learned test-taking abilities a pronounced grade-based advantage. While this benefits them in the short term, this does not necessarily translate to an applicable advantage in life beyond the classroom. Thus, students who typically excel on quizzes and exams may not have effectively learned essential knowledge and skills needed for future academic and professional pursuits. Alternatively, students who struggle to succeed on quizzes and exams may be lacking authentic opportunities in class to demonstrate the knowledge and skills they have acquired over time.

Countless students battle debilitating test anxiety, which significantly hinders their performance in school. Week after week, they suffer (often in silence) as they prepare for quizzes and exams, doubting their ability to excel and facing an impending sense of doom as they anticipate failing another quiz or exam.

In this way, traditional assessment measures (and the activities designed to prepare students for them) often cater to a select group of students who have mastered the art of taking quizzes and exams while simultaneously discouraging and leaving behind learners who struggle with traditional assessment measures.

When educators provide authentic learning opportunities that effectively mirror everyday life beyond classroom settings (unlike quizzes and exams), all learners benefit from meaningful, future-focused learning. Authentic academic endeavors ultimately promote a strengths-based learning environment, as students thrive through opportunities to showcase their development of future-focused knowledge and skills, rather than being evaluated on their ability to memorize material and to effectively navigate a quiz or exam.

The following formula for authentic learning is discussed in greater depth in the coming sections of this chapter: authentic issues + authentic audiences + authentic assessment = authentic learning experiences (Alaniz, 2021).

ADDRESSING AUTHENTIC ISSUES

As they seek to lead meaningful lives, adults engage in innumerable decision-making and problem-solving processes throughout each day. Along the way, they uncover solutions to countless real-life issues. Yet many of today's students struggle with problem-solving endeavors.

According to Alaniz and Cerling (2023),

> This may be that many are seldom exposed to substantial opportunities to tackle meaningful issues and to solve significant problems. Students spend the majority of their waking hours in classroom settings; their time devoted to schooling occupies a sizable percentage of highly pivotal years. For this reason, it is tremendously important that learners confront and engage in problem-solving opportunities during their years spent in school. (p. 53)

Gerald Aungst (2015), an educational author whose areas of specialization include digital literacy, gifted education, and mathematics curriculum development, wrote the book *Five Principles of the Modern Mathematics Classroom.* Aungst offers five steps toward cultivating a problem-solving culture in classroom settings: conjecture, communication, collaboration, chaos, and celebration.

An edWeb (2014) webinar highlighting Aungst's work features various insights regarding problem-solving opportunities that reach beyond curricular content in mathematical lessons. Aungst explains that instead of needing more individuals who excel at math, the world needs more people who are skilled at problem-solving. In other words, the world needs more innovators. In the words of Alaniz and Cerling (2023),

> Instead of viewing difficult problems as unsolvable, innovators seek out problems and attempt to solve them before anyone else recognizes that the problem even existed in the first place. Instead of endeavoring to offer solutions every time a problem presents itself, insightful educators avoid presenting an answer at the conclusion of each unit or lesson. As an alternative, they ask students to describe what they believe to be a potential answer, how they discovered a solution, and whether other solutions exist. Assessment experiences should include opportunities to seek out and uncover problems to solve. (p. 53)

In conjunction with Aungst's (2015) five principles, a helpful digital resource to support learning experiences involving the "conjecture" component is Data.gov (http://data.gov). As learners explore and interact with unfamiliar data, they may be prompted to draw a conclusion or form an opinion based off incomplete information.

Figure 5.1. http://data.gov

As they engage in the "communication" piece of Aungst's five principles, students practice explaining their thinking, ultimately developing their content knowledge. As learners describe the solutions they have formulated through their own words, they build useful skills for the future, no matter the professional opportunities they will one day pursue. Tools to support practice with effective communication include Piktochart (https://piktochart .com/) and Infogram (https://infogram.com/).

Figure 5.2. https://piktochart.com/

Figure 5.3. https://infogram.com/

The "collaboration" principle affects countless areas of life each day, as real-life problem-solving opportunities often rely upon collaboration. As students work together to engage in problem-solving experiences, they consider the perspectives of others, ultimately taking part in reciprocal learning endeavors. Countless digital tools and resources support collaborative problem-solving opportunities within the classroom, including cloud-based Google products such as Google Docs, Google Slides, and Google Sheets, as well as Office 365 products including Microsoft Word, Microsoft PowerPoint, and Microsoft Excel.

The "chaos" element builds upon the complicated nature of problem-solving endeavors. Acknowledging that problem solving may be messy, educators should provide learners with opportunities to struggle with problems in meaningful ways, thus making classroom experiences more relatable to everyday life, which is not often straightforward.

Finally, as described by Alaniz and Cerling (2023),

> The "celebration" component includes opportunities to empha-size students' development and successes, in addition to set-backs that will ultimately bring about new growth. Effective educators validate learners' efforts, not simply their correct answers. Students should be encouraged to persevere, even when their initial answers are incorrect. In her book entitled *Grit: The Power of Passion and Perseverance*, Duckworth (2016) identified the importance of both passion and perseverance in meeting goals. Effective educators establish a culture in which they and their students learn and grow in the face of setbacks. In the words of notable leadership author and renowned speaker John Maxwell, "Fail early, fail often, but always fail forward." (p. 55)

COMMUNICATING WITH AUTHENTIC AUDIENCES

Authentic learning experiences encourage students to share their newfound knowledge and skills, inspiring them to design their best work before presenting their creations to an audience. When learners realize that their work will be viewed by others beside their teacher, this knowledge typically motivates them to produce the most excellent possible artifacts of learning to share. As the modern world becomes more and more connected across time and space, innovative digital tools and resources offer increasingly accessible and effective platforms for students to display their work among real-life audience members.

A first step toward finding an appropriate audience involves reflecting upon the desired results of an assignment and artic-ulating key student learning outcomes. Next, teachers should decide upon an appropriate format (or various formats) for the assignment. This might include inviting students to collabora-tively solve a community issue through applying concepts they have learned in their social studies class. They might also explore issues surrounding current events discussed throughout their history lessons. When educators place student learning outcomes as the focal point of creative processes, appropriate audiences more naturally come to light.

The significance of offering students meaningful opportunities to share their learning with diverse audiences is discussed in Alaniz's *Collegial Coaching: Mentoring for Knowledge and Skills That Transfer to Real-World Applications* (2021):

> Authentic audiences should vary from project to project, providing students with opportunities to apply developing skills in the presence of different groups of people. Teachers may begin by seeking familiar audience members, such as family, friends, or others who already have an interest in students' lives. Learners might also present their creations to others within the school setting, such as students in other classes or grade levels as well as administrators or instructional support specialists. It may also be helpful to seek the support of experts in the field. For example, students working on an impressionist painting project in art class might host a gallery walk and invite a local artist to tour the exhibit. (p. 97)

Mathtrain.TV (http://mathtrain.tv/) offers an impactful example of the power of exposure to authentic audiences to encourage learners to create excellent artifacts of learning. The students at Lincoln Middle School in Santa Monica, California, collaboratively design math screencasts and share them through their website; these engaging student-created tutorials have been viewed by tens of thousands of people across the globe. As learners produce these popular videos, they engage in critical thinking to effectively communicate problem-solving strategies.

Figure 5.4.http://mathtrain.tv/

At the time of publication, Mathtrain.TV's videos have been accessed by more than sixty thousand individuals worldwide. What a powerful indicator of the difference sharing with authentic audiences makes in the lives of students! These students must feel an immense sense of empowerment and purpose as their videos are accessed by individuals they will likely never even meet and yet still support in learning new math concepts.

Creating Impactful Authentic Assessments
As described by Alaniz (2021),

> [Authentic assessments provide] a revealing glimpse of what learners actually know and what they can actually do, rather than simply showcasing how skillfully students can take quizzes or exams. Authentic assessments provide opportunities for learners to create novel end products, rather than simply requiring that they consume information for the purpose of regurgitating it while taking a quiz or exam. (p. 98)

In fact, within the Master of Science in Learning, Technology, and Design program at Houston Christian University, the university at which the author teaches, none of the courses include quizzes or exams. Rather, they entail various authentic assessment experiences applicable to students' current or future endeavors as instructional designers. Throughout every course, students design artifacts of learning as a means of providing evidence of their grasp of key student learning outcomes. By beginning with the end in mind, students create innovative digital tools as well as educational resources to utilize in their current and/or future professional contexts.

The aspiring instructional designers within the program intentionally plan and execute assessment pieces, intrinsically motivated in knowing that their learning throughout the program will benefit the students within their spheres of influence. As a result, finalized products demonstrate exemplary instructional design endeavors, and students typically express excitement in sharing their online portfolios with others. In fact, many graduates add a portfolio link in their email signature or place a QR code within their resume to point others in their professional networks to their portfolios. Many students have received professional awards, new jobs, or promotions based upon their excellent online portfolios.

The following QR code links to a digital portfolio created by Master of Science in Learning, Technology, and Design graduate Julie Blackwell (https://julieblackwell.weebly.com/portfolio .html).

Figure 5.5. https://julieblackwell.weebly.com/portfolio.html

QUESTIONS FOR REFLECTION

Each day contains exactly 24 hours—that's 1,440 minutes. A relatively small investment of 15 to 30 minutes per day devoted to deeply, genuinely reflecting on the following questions will undoubtedly reap long-lasting dividends. Heartfelt reflection fuels the journey toward developing a learning community built on strengths, positively impacting the lives of countless students. The more honest each answer, the greater the potential impact. Now is the time to tackle technological change!

- Reflecting upon the school or district setting in which you teach and/or lead, how has technological innovation changed teaching and learning experiences?

- Reflecting upon the school or district setting in which you teach and/or lead, has technological innovation provided new opportunities for all learners to find success? If so, how? If not, why might this be?

- As you consider the formula for authentic learning (Alaniz, 2021) provided within this chapter (authentic audiences + authentic issues + authentic assessment), how might this impact the students under your influence to transition from consumers of information to creators of new learning experiences?

- How might authentic learning opportunities provide an advantage to students who struggle with testing anxiety or find more traditional assessment methods especially challenging?

- Share at least one idea for incorporating authentic learning with the learners you teach. If you support or lead teachers, how might you help them to incorporate authentic learning within their teaching endeavors?

Essential Ideas to Remember

Authentic academic endeavors represent a hallmark of strengths-based teaching and learning environments. Such educational experiences ineradicably impact not only success during students' schooling years but also success in their lives well beyond graduation. As teachers develop and implement learning opportunities that apply to the everyday lives of students, learners acquire transferable knowledge and skills. The following represents a key formula for purposeful learning: authentic issues + authentic audiences + authentic assessment = authentic learning experiences (Alaniz, 2021).

Such learning experiences provide opportunities for all learners to thrive rather than limiting students who suffer from testing anxiety. As learners transition from consumers of information to creators of new learning experiences, the sky is the limit. In such educational environments, students are more likely to succeed in school. Even more importantly, they are also more likely develop a love for learning that will last a lifetime!

REFERENCES

Alaniz, K. (2021). *Collegial coaching: Mentoring for knowledge and skills that transfer to real-world applications.* Lanham, MD: Rowman & Littlefield Education.

Alaniz, K., & Cerling, K. (2023). *Authentic assessment in action: An everyday guide for bringing learning to life through meaningful assessment.* Lanham, MD: Rowman & Littlefield Education.

Aungst, G. (2015). *Five principles of the modern mathematics classroom: Creating a culture of innovative thinking.* Thousand Oaks, CA: Corwin.

Duckworth, A. (2016). *Grit: The power of passion and perseverance* (Vol. 234). New York: Scribner.

edWeb (2014, August 20). Creating a culture of problem solving in your school or classroom. https://home.edweb.net/creating-culture-problem-solving-school-classroom/.

Herring, M. C., Koehler, M. J., & Mishra, P. (2016). *Handbook of technological pedagogical content knowledge (TPACK) for educators* (2nd ed.). New York: Routledge.

Koehler, M. J. (2012, September 24). *TPACK explained.* https://matt-koehler.com/tpack2/tpack-explained/.

Koehler, M. J., & Mishra, P. (2009). What is technological pedagogical content knowledge? *Contemporary Issues in Technology and Teacher Education, 9*(1), 60–70.

Shulman, L. S. (1986). Those who understand: Knowledge growth in teaching. *Educational Researcher, 15*(2), 4–14.

Embracing Lifelong Learning

The Power of Purposeful Professional Development

If you are not willing to learn, no one can help you.
If you are willing to learn, no one can stop you.

—ZIG ZIGLAR

AS TEACHERS FACE INCREASING DEMANDS FOR ACCOUNTABILITY and progressively limited time to spare, professional development may naturally be viewed as another box to check off on an extensive to-do list. Yet when educators facilitate reflective communities of practice that focus on strengths-based teaching and learning, they often find that their implementation of such approaches becomes more natural and purposeful, producing powerful results. This chapter provides feasible strategies for cultivating strengths-based communities of practice in which such strategies can be explored, discussed, and built upon, ultimately impacting student lives for the better.

QUESTIONS TO CONSIDER WHEN CULTIVATING A STRENGTHS-BASED CULTURE

Not surprisingly, strengths-based approaches to professional development extend far beyond educational settings. The most effective leaders across all sectors seek out methods for focusing upon strengths as a means of developing a more encouraging, productive, positive workplace in which employees value and strive for consistent growth.

While some leaders waste valuable time and money focusing on the weaknesses of those within their organization and devoting training efforts to those areas, this tactic may pave the way toward mediocre wins at best. Alternatively, a strengths-based approach supports leaders in ensuring that employees' efforts are not wasted. Though capitalizing on strengths, work is more collaborative and ultimately more meaningful.

The Center for Management and Organization Effectiveness (n.d.) offers helpful questions leaders should ask themselves when seeking to implement a strengths-based approach to leadership. Many of the questions offered effectively apply to academic settings, including the following:

- Does my company [or in this case, school] have systems in place to study our best performers?
- How can we ensure that the right people with the right talents are placed in the right roles?
- Are we able to replicate excellent performance company-wide [or school- or district-wide]?
- Are we providing opportunities for star performers to progress through the ranks?
- Do we build, appreciate, and communicate excellence at every level? (para. 8)

The CMOE also offers questions leaders should ask those they lead, describing the importance of this process:

Once those principles and processes are in place, shining a light on what your employees do best is the next step to implementing a strengths-based approach to development. You can certainly make your own assumptions based on observations and performance reviews. However, having a face-to-face conversation will open your eyes (and your employee's eyes) to much more untapped potential that can be put to good use.

Ask the people you lead the following questions and make detailed notes you can refer to later:

- What do you enjoy most in your day-to-day work activities?
- What part of your role energizes you?
- What have your greatest accomplishments been in the last six months?
- Have you gathered feedback about how to best apply your talents at work?

If your employees are involved in work activities and tasks that they gravitate towards and naturally do well, you will notice that they have a positive attitude, are more willing to contribute, and are on the path to becoming star performers. (paras. 9–11)

A TRANSFORMATIVE PLAN OF ACTION

Building upon the importance of insightful questions, in her article "Transforming Schools Through Strengths-Based PD" (2016), Laura McBain, director of External Relations and Education Leadership Academy at High Tech High Graduate School of Education, asks the following question: "What would professional development look like if we focused on our greatest strengths as opposed to our greatest deficits?" (para. 1).

McBain's article (2016) describes an inspiring journey toward strengths-based professional development at a struggling Chicago school:

Transformative change in schools begins with the recognition that every participant has a best practice to share. It is about helping teachers and schools become the best versions of themselves. This was the mindset I started with when I began working with an urban school called Chicago Tech Academy in the South Side area of Chicago. In May of 2014, the school was on the brink of being closed by Chicago Public Schools. Low test scores, low staff morale and low student engagement laid heavy on a school already struggling with the violence and equity issues prevalent in Chicago. If students wanted to use the restroom, they were escorted by a security guard. (paras. 2–3)

In this particular school, teachers over time developed a familiarity with "experts" from outside their school community dropping in to tell them how to instruct more effectively or how to "fix their school." Thus, in thinking through more impactful and lasting ways to support the teachers and staff, McBain and her team intentionally focused on celebrations.

In McBain's words,

We wanted the professional development to be a rebirth of their passion for teaching and their commitment to equity, rather than a laundry list of things to fix. Instead, we thought about the assumptions of appreciative inquiry which suggest that:

- In every society, organization or group, something works;
- What we focus on becomes our reality;
- Reality is created in the moment, and there are multiple realities. If we carry parts of the past forward, they should be what is best about the past;
- It is important to value differences; and
- The language we use creates our reality.

We began the work of designing a disruptive and celebratory professional development program. Our aim was not merely to shift the pedagogical practices of teachers but rather to create a program that cultivated a growth mindset toward teaching and learning. (paras. 3–6)

Faculty, staff, and school leaders worked in groups to explore, interview, and create artifacts that signified what they were learning. At the conclusion of the day, they reflected upon new insights gained. They delved deeply into their learning from each exercise and ultimately acknowledged that certain assumptions regarding students were not accurate.

McBain (2016) offers this description of her insights gained as a result of this experience:

> For me, this opening day activity served two purposes. First, it acted as a unifying experience for the staff to help bring them together. Second, it served to disrupt the staff's current thinking about what teaching and learning was supposed to look and feel like in schools . . . we set about creating structures in the ongoing staff meetings that would engender reflection and community building in the hopes that we would create an adult learning where staff felt valued and were free to take risks. We hoped that if the staff were able to feel a sense of celebration and accomplishment about their own work, they would bring this same feeling to their students. (paras. 8, 10)

Within two years, evidence of the effectiveness of these strategies to transform the culture abounded throughout the school. At the time of publication of the article, attendance was hovering at 90 percent, 100 percent of seniors were preparing to start their academic internships, visitors were consistently being greeted by student ambassadors, and students' artifacts of learning were covering hallways throughout the school.

McBain (2016) describes how gratifying it feels to witness this type of change within a school setting:

Working with this school and its teachers over the past few years has been tremendously rewarding. It has equally challenged and reaffirmed my belief that if we want to change schools, we have to start with the adults. No school is a masterpiece, but if we can design professional development that allows adults to become the best versions of themselves, then perhaps then we can create classrooms that allow students to be the best versions of themselves as well. (para. 13)

Although this type of transformation requires that faculty, staff, and school leaders work collaboratively and consistently to progress toward a strengths-based culture, such results are not elusive. McBain (2016) offers practical strategies for cultivating a culture focused on strengths within any school setting:

Offer Disruptive Professional Development Learning Opportunities to Staff

- Send staff to museums to see how work is curated.
- Conduct a staff professional development day where every staff member does an internship in an area outside education.
- If practicing project-based learning, ask teachers to do the project themselves first before they do it with students.

Create a Sense of Belonging

- Start staff meetings with appreciative inquiry and celebrations.
- Create a collegial coaching program where teachers visit and provide peer feedback.
- Create your own promising practices blog or bulletin board that shares the best practices from all the staff.

Making Meaning

- Have teachers create their own personal learning plans focused on their own success and challenges.

- Use protocols—such as project tunings or consultancies—with staff, allowing teachers to examine problems of practice.

- Instead of a formal evaluation system, allow teachers to share their learning from the year in a presentation of learning to their peers. (McBain, 2016, paras. 13–15)

As teachers, staff members, and school leaders collaborate to create a culture of celebration, students will undeniably sense positive changes in the adults leading their learning experiences and will also likely find opportunities to celebrate their growth and learning as well.

QUESTIONS FOR REFLECTION

Each day contains exactly 24 hours—that's 1,440 minutes. A relatively small investment of 15 to 30 minutes per day devoted to deeply, genuinely reflecting on the following questions will undoubtedly reap long-lasting dividends. Heartfelt reflection fuels the journey toward developing a learning community built on strengths, positively impacting the lives of countless students. The more honest each answer, the greater the potential impact. Now is the time to embrace lifelong learning!

- Reflecting upon the school or district setting in which you teach and/or lead, what would it look like to offer disruptive and celebratory professional development learning opportunities to staff?

- Reflecting upon the school or district setting in which you teach and/or lead, how might you help in creating a sense of belonging among faculty, staff, students, and other stake-holders (such as parents and community volunteers)?

- Reflecting upon the school or district setting in which you teach and/or lead, what would it look like for faculty and staff to take the initiative in making meaning of their growth and celebrating successes? How might you help facilitate this process?

- Other than the questions for leaders offered in this chapter, what questions should be asked about your school or district setting?

- Other than the questions for leaders offered in this chapter, what questions should be asked of the faculty, staff, and students within your school or district?

ESSENTIAL IDEAS TO REMEMBER

For some schools and districts, a strengths-based approach to teaching seems to develop more naturally. Within other schools and districts, it feels as though a great deal of work is yet to be done. No matter how near or far attainment of this type of environment seems, a strengths-based, collaborative culture in which celebration is the norm is within reach for any school or district. As leaders reflect upon and respond to essential questions and as faculty, staff, and leaders work in partnership to leverage opportunities for intentional collaboration and celebration, anything is possible!

REFERENCES

Center for Management and Organization Effectiveness (n.d.). Employee development: Consider a strengths-based approach. *Center for Management and Organization Effectiveness.* https://cmoe.com/blog/employee -development-strengths-based-approach/.

McBain, L. (2016, April 28). Transforming schools through strengths-based PD. *Getting Smart.* https://www.gettingsmart.com/2016/04/28/transforming -schools-through-strengths-based-pd/.

Reflecting on the Road Less Traveled

The Joy-Filled Journey Ahead

We must look on our children in need not as problems but as individuals with potential. . . .
I would hope we could find creative ways to draw out of our children the good that there is in each of them.
—Archbishop Desmond Tutu

Although the United States is known for individuality, US school systems are surprisingly cookie-cutter in many ways. Education for the masses has created derivative approaches that may stifle students' creativity and progress in learning, placing them in categories with narrowly tailored metrics of intelligence that label and stigmatize them.

Considering how many schools operate, it would seem that the definition of intelligence and success is making the fewest mistakes on often subjective and narrow measures. This chapter offers practical steps and questions for reflection to incorporate. They support faculty, staff, and school/district leaders in employing an individualized, strengths-based approach to education that provides avenues for student creativity to flourish and for students (and their teachers) to ultimately and joyfully reach their fullest potential.

GUIDING PRINCIPLES OF STRENGTH-BASED EDUCATIONAL APPROACHES

Strength-based approaches are unique in educational settings for a variety of reasons, including that they do not focus exclusively on procedures; rather, strengths-based educational practices draw from techniques and knowledge as foundational keys to change. Strengths-based teaching and learning centers upon the belief that every student holds the potential for their own unique transformational processes. Such approaches involve not only teaching students as they seem willing to learn; often, even before this occurs, they entail preparing students to learn effectively.

In the words of the Alberta Mentoring Partnership (n.d.),

> A strength-based approach involves a different way of thinking about students and of interpreting the ways they cope with life challenges. With a strength-based mindset, one engages to invite curious exploration of "what can be" based upon a clear set of values and attitudes.

The following principles are the foundation for guiding and implementing strength-based practice (O'Connell, 2006; Rapp & Goscha, 2006; McCashen, 2005):

1. An absolute belief that every student has potential. Their unique strengths and capabilities will determine their evolving story and define who they are rather than what they're not.
2. What we focus on becomes a student's reality. Focus on what a student can do rather than on what they can't do. See challenges as opportunities to explore, not something to avoid. Start with small successes and build upon them to create hope and optimism.

3. Being mindful that the language we use creates a reality—both for the educators and the student (e.g., saying "It looks like you tried doing this exercise another way; let's see how it worked for you." As opposed to saying, "Did you not hear what I told the other students?").

4. Believe that change is inevitable, and all students can and will be successful. All students have the urge to succeed, to explore the world around them, and to contribute to their communities.

5. Positive change occurs in the context of authentic relationships. Students need to know school staff care and will be there for them unconditionally.

6. What a student thinks about themselves, and their reality is primary. Therefore, educators must value and start the change process with what is important to the student. It's the student's story that's important, not the expert's.

7. Students have more confidence in journeying to the future (or the unknown) when they are encouraged to start with what they already know.

8. Capacity building is a process and a goal. Change is a dynamic process. Your ongoing support of this change has a cumulative effect.

9. It is important to value differences and the essential need to collaborate. Effective change is a collaborative, inclusive and participatory process. (pp. 4–5)

Cultivating Students' Preparation for the Future

When implemented effectively and consistently, strengths-based practices serve to prepare students for the successful pursuit of new professional and personal endeavors well beyond their schooling years. Lopez and Louis (2009) offer practical principles of strengths-based teaching and learning that can effectively support educators in cultivating student engagement, learner well-being, retention in school, and readiness for the future:

- Measure student strengths: Provide learners with a survey comprised of questions that support them in identifying their key strengths (Schreiner, 2013). Engage students in a discussion focusing on their experience taking and reflecting upon the survey, or offer individual meetings with learners to support them in reflecting upon their unique interpretations of the results.

- Create individualized learning opportunities: Offer differentiated, personalized learning experiences that allow students to leverage their strengths through unique demonstrations of their learning. Authentic learning experiences naturally make this possible for students. Such opportunities are discussed more fully in Chapter 5, which includes the formula for authentic learning, or authentic audiences + authentic issues + authentic assessment (Alaniz, 2021).

- Help students network with strength supporters: Support students through providing mentorship experiences or designing cohort-based collaborative class groupings that offer help and feedback from peers.

- Provide opportunities where students can develop and integrate new strengths: Assist students in developing new strengths by designing learning opportunities that will allow them to explore and practice new skills. Support learners in making connections between their personal goals, their strengths, and areas in which they can grow. This will enable them to build confidence, independence, and a sense of connection between these various elements of their development as individuals.

- Advise for strengths development: Through intentional practice and engagement, support learners in considering their responsibility in developing their own strengths. Advise students in developing new strategies or accessing previously untapped resources in building their strengths.

Offer one-on-one consultations or one-minute reflection activities that encourage students to articulate their strengths.

As described by the Alberta Mentoring Partnership, "The strength-based approach has a contagious quality and makes deep, intuitive sense to those who reflect a 'half cup full' attitude in life" (n.d., p. 13). Educators who consistently practice the art of leveraging and capitalizing on students' strengths rather than emphasizing their weaknesses hold the power to entirely alter learners' educational experiences for the better. Strengths-based approaches to education breathe new life into classrooms settings, encouraging each student to realize and ultimately to reach their fullest potential.

Teachers and administrators committed to focusing on strengths-based approaches to education typically experience far greater joy in the journey toward student success. As they embrace attitudes and approaches that reflect a genuine sense of value in the worth of others, the profession of education becomes much more than a duty or a job. Instead, it becomes a profound calling and quite possibly even the adventure of a lifetime.

A learning community built on strengths may not yet be the norm in the majority of academic settings, but such an environment is well within reach. The commitment of a single educator to strengths-based teaching and learning holds the power to transform student lives and school cultures within the classroom and beyond, ultimately impacting the world in ways that cannot be measured.

QUESTIONS FOR REFLECTION

Each day contains exactly 24 hours—that's 1,440 minutes. A relatively small investment of 15 to 30 minutes per day devoted to deeply, genuinely reflecting on the below questions will undoubtedly reap long-lasting dividends. Heartfelt reflection fuels the journey toward developing a learning community built on strengths, positively impacting the lives of countless students. The more honest each answer, the greater the potential impact. Now is the time to reflect on the road less traveled toward a strengths-based approach to education!

- Of the practices mentioned within this chapter, which seems to be most easily implemented within your school or district? Why?

- Of the practices mentioned within this chapter, which seems to be most challenging to implement within your school or district? Why?

- In your own words, how might a strengths-based approach to teaching and learning support students in preparing for the future, both personally and professionally?

- How does a strength-approach mirror or differ from the setting in which you currently teach and/or lead? What next steps need to be taken in the journey toward strengths-based education?

- Who can you invite to join you on this journey?

ESSENTIAL IDEAS TO REMEMBER

The profession of teaching represents both an art and a science. Educators masterfully showcase their artistry when they meet students where they are and inspire them to reach their fullest potential. At the same time, teaching involves successfully incorporating research-driven instructional strategies to facilitate opportunities for students to develop and master new knowledge and skills. While teaching is among the most rewarding professions a person can pursue, it can also be among the most challenging.

Strengths-based approaches to teaching and learning bring newfound joy to the journey as the best in students is celebrated and built upon. No matter an educators' prior training or experiences, no matter the students in a class, no matter the resources available, this approach is highly possible and indescribably transformative. There is no better time to begin the great adventure toward strengths-based education than now. The lives of students—and the lives of their teachers—will forever be impacted for the better!

REFERENCES

Alaniz, K. (2021). *Collegial coaching: Mentoring for knowledge and skills that transfer to real-world applications.* Lanham, MD: Rowman & Littlefield Education.

Alberta Mentoring Partnership (n.d.). *Creating strengths-based classrooms and schools: A practice guide for schools.* www.albertamentors.ca.

Lopez, S. J., & Louis, M. C. (2009). The principles of strengths-based education. *Journal of College and Character, 10*(4).

McCashen, W. (2005) *The strengths approach.* Victoria: St. Luke's Innovative Resources.

O'Connell, D. (2006). *Brief literature review on strength-based teaching and counseling.* Research and draft prepared for the Metropolitan Action Committee on Violence Against Women and Children (METRAC).

Rapp, C. & Goscha, R. J. (2006) *The strengths model: Case management with people suffering severe and persistent mental illness.* New York: Oxford Press.

Schreiner, L. A. (2013). Strengths-based advising. *Academic Advising Approaches: Strategies That Teach Students to Make the Most of College,* 105–20.

About the Author

Katie Alaniz, EdD, serves as director of the Center for Learning Innovations and Teaching Excellence (C-LITE) at Houston Christian University, where she also teaches undergraduate and graduate education courses within the College of Education and Behavioral Sciences. As a teacher and digital learning specialist for nearly two decades in both public and private schools, Dr. Alaniz guides educators as they meaningfully integrate digital tools and resources within their classrooms. Dr. Alaniz has authored or coauthored a number of books, including *Naturalizing Digital Immigrants: The Power of Collegial Coaching for Technology Integration*; *Digital Media in Today's Classroom: The Potential for Meaningful Teaching, Learning, and Assessment*; *Collegial Coaching: Mentoring for Knowledge and Skills That Transfer to Real-World Applications*; *The Maximizer Mindset: Work Less, Achieve More, Spread Joy*; and *Authentic Assessment in Action: An Everyday Guide for Bringing Learning to Life through Meaningful Assessment*. Additionally, she has published academic articles on a range of topics and presented at a variety of educational conferences in the United States and abroad. Her primary research interests include authentic assessment, digital learning, collegial coaching, and teacher education. Dr. Alaniz and her husband, Steven, reside in Houston and together enjoy serving their community through a nonprofit outreach program called Apartment Life.